"Linda Loosli is my 'go to' gal for any organization, knowledge or skill that I need for all things preparedness and emergency! Her passion for preparedness is clearly proven in her well-researched writing."

-STACY LYN HARRIS, author of *Recipes and Tips for Sustainable Living* and GameAndGarden.com

"Linda Loosli has become one of the leading voices in the industry and I'm proud to call her my friend and colleague."

-MICHAEL PRUNTY, TheBackyardPioneer.com

"Linda Loosli is one of the rock stars of the preparedness world. Whether you're storing food for a zombie apocalypse or simply want a well-stocked pantry, Linda's down-to-earth practical advice is for you. May *Prepare Your Family for Survival* be the first of many books from this author."

-PJ SCHOTT, SurvivalForBlondes.com

"I sometimes stand in awe and amazement at the amount of knowledge Linda Loosli has when it comes to emergency preparedness. She is my go-to source for all things preparedness and food storage. When I think of being prepared, I think of Linda Loosli."

-DUSTIN KIRBY, Sales and Marketing Manager at Cox's Honey

"Linda Loosli does an excellent job explaining how to be prepared and use dried foods in everyday cooking! She gives easy-to-follow instructions, helps readers understand what to stock up on, and provides great cooking tips."

-LAURA RANTALA, Sales and Marketing Manager at North Bay Trading Company

"Coming from a background filled with ready-made meals and eating out, I had a lot to learn about building and using a pantry. Linda's lifelong preparedness and food storage experience is evident in her practical, easy-to-follow advice. Thanks to her, my family is now eating delicious homemade meals—and I look like a rock-star mom."

-JULIE SCZERBINSKI, author of *The Survival Savvy Family* and HomeReadyHome.com

PAGE STREET
PUBLISHING CO.

HOW TO BE READY
FOR ANY EMERGENCY OR
DISASTER SITUATION

PREPARE YOUR FAMILY FOR SURVIVAL

LINDA LOOSLI, FOUNDER OF FOOD STORAGE MOMS

PAGE STREET
PUBLISHING CO.

First published in 2015 by
Page Street Publishing Co.
27 Congress Street, Suite 103
Salem, MA 01970
www.pagestreetpublishing.com

Distributed by Macmillan, sales in Canada by The Canadian Manda Group.

18   17   16   15   1   2   3   4   5

ISBN-13: 978-1-62414-175-1
ISBN-10: 1-62414-175-7

Library of Congress Control Number: 2015947538

Cover and book design by Page Street Publishing Co.
Illustrations by Robert Brandt

Printed and bound in the U.S.A.

Page Street is proud to be a member of 1% for the Planet. Members donate one percent of
their sales to one or more of the over 1,500 environmental and sustainability charities across
the globe who participate in this program.

DEDICATED TO THE FIVE MOST IMPORTANT PEOPLE IN MY LIFE, MARK, ALLI, STACIE, HEIDI, AND CAMILLE, MY LOVING FAMILY MEMBERS. YOU ARE THE REASON I PREPARE.

CONTENTS

INTRODUCTION
FROM MY HOME TO YOURS

When I was 16, I went to live with my aunt and her family outside of Chicago. My aunt had a new baby, and I had come to help out for six months. Well, you probably know that Chicago winters can be pretty harsh. One morning I was getting ready to leave for school when we learned that it had been canceled because of the snow and ice. One day became two days, then three, and then several days. School ended up being canceled for two weeks.

Now my aunt wasn't accustomed to storing very much food in her pantry. As I recall, there were just a few cans of vegetables and a jar of peanut butter, so my cousin and I were sent out to pick up some groceries. When we got to the store we found the shelves nearly bare. Because road conditions were so bad and deliveries couldn't be made, restrictions were placed on how much food you could buy. We were allowed one pound of hamburger meat and one quart of milk a week.

I can't begin to tell you how miserable I was. The roads were slippery and the temperatures frigid, and having grown up in Las Vegas, I didn't own a coat, let alone boots and gloves. My cousin and I trudged home in the bitter cold with our allotted food items, and I remember thinking, *What are we going to eat?* During those weeks a fear of hunger consumed my thoughts.

One day walking home from the store, I vowed to myself that when I got married and had children, this would never happen to my family. I never wanted to experience this fear again or let my family feel the pangs of hunger that gnawed at my belly. And I kept that promise.

Years later after my husband and I got married and started our family, I planted a huge garden—the biggest one in the neighborhood. I canned everything, including apricots, peaches, pears, green beans, salsa, and spaghetti sauce. And when my girls were old enough, they helped. We dehydrated fruit and vegetables and even made juice from grapes. I had been fortunate to learn these skills at *my* mother's side. She filled her pantry with foods that she had canned herself, and she always made bread. I remember as a little girl watching her add the flour, yeast, water, and other ingredients into a big silver bowl, mix them, and knead the dough with her strong hands. Today, I'm proud to say that I've been making bread myself for 40 years.

And I've canned and stored plenty of food. But I started thinking about our neighborhood and our church community and wondering how other people were doing with emergency preparedness. I knew I had enough food stored for myself and my husband, Mark, but I couldn't feed an entire neighborhood if there were a crisis that lasted for any length of time. I wanted to make sure my community was okay, so I decided to see what was going on with food storage and emergency preparedness. I started posting on Facebook and encouraging discussion, and I learned that most people didn't even know where to begin, and they were nervous about it, so I decided to offer classes in my home. Every Wednesday I'd post to Facebook. I didn't charge for the classes. We'd start at 5:30, and I'd offer samples of food to try, like freeze-dried green beans (people were amazed at how good they tasted). In my early classes I showed "my students" how to put together a binder where they could store important documents and information that they'd want to grab and take with them if they ever needed to evacuate their home, and then I went on to teach about food storage. Sometimes I'd have six women show up; other times it would be just a mom and a grandma. Everyone was extremely grateful.

I saw that there was a great need for this information and I suspected it went way beyond my local community. In May of 2012 I started my blog, Food Storage Moms, so that I could reach many more people. As word of my blog got around, food storage companies started to contact me and ask me to review their products—I've tried 99 percent of what's available. I keep up with what's new by reading and attending conferences so that I can share the latest information.

Food storage and emergency preparedness are a little scary and overwhelming for many people. The words conjure up worries not only about natural disasters, like hurricanes and wildfires, but man-made ones as well, like terrorism and war. I am not a doomsday thinker. I don't believe the world is going to end tomorrow or the day after tomorrow or next year or the year after. I do know that bad stuff happens, whether it's an ice storm that immobilizes your town and creates food shortages, as was my childhood experience, or a hurricane that blows out power for weeks or even a job loss that severely limits your financial resources.

I want you to be prepared for the unexpected. I want to help you and people everywhere become self-reliant. Food storage and emergency preparedness are easy, and even fun. My wish for you and your family is that you never go hungry or thirsty or cold; never have to worry about when you'll have your next meal—that wish is the heart of this book. I invite you inside just as I invited my neighbors into my home. Come on in and let's get started.

Linda Loosli

ARE YOU PREPARED?

I watched a television newscast last winter reporting on unusually heavy snowstorms in the southeastern United States where power lines were being torn down by broken tree branches. Even the power poles were breaking from the weight of the snow on the lines. About 184,000 people were without power for days.

More recently, I learned of a tragic tale out of Northern Utah where a major snowstorm hit, and wild winds flipped dozens of semis on their sides. Tree branches broke and ripped down power lines as they dropped to the ground. In one neighborhood, a huge old tree was uprooted and sent crashing into a home, splitting the house in two and killing one of the family members as he slept. Who would have thought that a beautiful tree, one that had been part of the family landscape for so many years, would prove to be the tool the vicious winds would use to destroy a beloved home?

Sometimes, it's the earth that wreaks destruction. One night, a neighborhood north of Salt Lake City was awakened in the middle of the night by a landslide. Pelted by a heavy rainstorm, the denuded hill became unstable and gravity pulled the side of the hill right down and into the back of a home. Fortunately the family woke up when they heard the rumbling and were able to vacate in time to reach safety. Such a huge volume of dirt, mud, and boulders hit the home that it was totally destroyed.

Of course you remember Hurricane Sandy in 2012. Roughly 8 million people lost power up and down the eastern seaboard and as far west as Michigan, and hundreds of thousands of families didn't see their power restored for more than a week. Tens of thousands of homes were flooded or destroyed along the coast, businesses were ruined, and years later communities are still recovering.

Storms, hurricanes, wildfires, drought—the number of climate-related disasters around the world has climbed steeply over the past 25 years according to statistics from the United Nations International Strategy for Disaster Reduction, and scientists predict this rise to continue. Watch the news, and you see story after story not just of natural disasters like storms and earthquakes, but man-made horrors like riots, war, and terrorism.

Keep in mind, too, that a catastrophic event could even include the loss of a job. So many families struggle financially. Job security is a thing of the past, and older adults and those who have specialized skills for which demand has dwindled may have a tough time finding well-paying employment. If they've had to live paycheck-to-paycheck in their previous jobs, they may find themselves with little savings and struggling to feed their families.

Maybe you've experienced one of these events or you've been fortunate not to but you wonder how well you would survive in such a situation. I certainly did and so I became an expert at emergency preparedness. Now I go to bed every night knowing that my husband and I will be able to take care of ourselves in any emergency. You can, too. Begin with an honest self-assessment. Ask yourself these questions.

IF THE WATER LINES WERE DAMAGED OR YOUR WELL BECAME CONTAMINATED AND WATER WASN'T COMING INTO YOUR HOME, WHERE WOULD YOU TURN FOR CLEAN DRINKABLE WATER?

You can survive only days without water. How many days depends upon the conditions. If it's hot and humid, you'll sweat more and lose water faster than if temperatures are moderate. In any emergency, at the bare minimum, you'll need drinking water for you and your family. But think about the other ways you use water. Macaroni and cheese out of a box isn't very tasty if it's not cooked with water. You need to wash your hands, and if water isn't available for several days, you'll want to at least take a sponge bath. Water storage is essential, and we'll talk about how much to store and how to store it—this is one item you don't want to scrimp on! I'll also show you a few ways to purify water so you can drink it.

IF YOU COULDN'T GET TO THE GROCERY STORE OR THE SUPERMARKET SHELVES WERE EMPTY, WOULD YOUR FAMILY HAVE ENOUGH FOOD TO LAST EVEN A WEEK?

I know people who do their weekly shopping on a Saturday or Sunday and still end up running to the store on Wednesday because they ran out of milk, eggs, or bread. This can be especially true of those who live in easy driving distance of their local supermarket. But even the store that's a mile down the road may be difficult to reach if roads become treacherous. Or there may be little food on your grocer's shelves after a natural disaster. It's best to stock up not just for the current week of meals but for longer in case of an emergency.

This doesn't mean spending thousands of dollars all at once and stacking tons of groceries in your basement. Food storage is a planned, gradual, cost-effective process. I will show you how to figure out what your family needs, how to purchase efficiently so you don't waste money on items that you won't eat or won't have a long shelf life, and how to store these foods so that you don't waste anything.

I've seen people purchase huge containers of wheat that they save for an emergency even though they don't regularly eat whole-wheat products. It would be hard on your digestive system if your emergency food plan is based mainly on food that you weren't accustomed to eating. Or consider the person who buys a year's supply of dehydrated vegetables and meats but doesn't store enough water to hydrate it. That food won't be very palatable, trust me! I've thought through all of this and carefully planned and mastered my own food storage, and I'll guide you step by step through a process that's cost effective, easy on your budget, and provides you with food that you'll enjoy eating if you are stranded at home.

IF THE POWER WENT OUT,
... HOW WOULD YOU PREPARE THE FOOD THAT YOU HAVE?
... WHAT WOULD YOU USE FOR LIGHT?
... HOW WOULD YOU STAY WARM IN THE COLD OR COOL DOWN IN THE HEAT?

Our energy needs are constant, as is the source—or so it seems. From switching on a light to running the furnace or gas heater, to recharging our cell phones, we use electricity all day long.

So what will you do when it goes off? If you have a gas stove, you may still be able to cook meals and heat water but if not, are you okay with eating cold food out of a can for days, possibly weeks, and taking cold sponge baths to keep clean? Do you have a good supply of fresh batteries for your flashlights or a large stash of candles and matches to provide some light when the sun sets? When the furnace goes cold or the air-conditioning dies, how will you stay comfortable? Fortunately, you have so many options for cooking, lighting, heating, and cooling—more than you may be aware of—and I will take you through those options and help you decide what's best for you, your family, and your home.

IF THERE WAS NO WATER COMING INTO YOUR HOME, HOW WOULD YOU AND YOUR FAMILY TAKE CARE OF YOUR PERSONAL HYGIENE NEEDS?

No water means no working toilet—another convenience we tend to take for granted. If you have a backyard, you might be able to go *au natural* or create a temporary makeshift outhouse. But what if the temperatures are below freezing or you rent an apartment or condo and don't have a backyard? This may not be the most appealing conversation to have, but the reality is that though the household plumbing may shut down, your body's plumbing keeps on running. I'll share a few innovative ways to solve your bathroom needs and take care of all your personal hygiene from washing your hands to even laundering your clothes if a power outage becomes lengthy.

IF YOUR FAMILY HAD TO EVACUATE YOUR HOME, WHERE WOULD YOU GO? WHAT SHOULD YOU TAKE WITH YOU?

Perhaps you and your family have a short-term emergency escape plan in case of a fire. You've discussed with your children how to leave the home safely and where to go to meet up. But are you prepared for evacuation in the case of a hurricane, raging wildfire, or some other natural disaster? Stop for a minute and imagine what you would do if the government ordered your town to leave immediately due to a fast-approaching threat. You'll need, at the very least, food, water, and important documents, and you'll need to grab them and go quickly. I'll help you create what's called a bug-out bag or 72-hour kit with what you'll need to carry you through three days away from home, and we'll talk about where to store it for easy access and how to keep everything in it current and fresh so you're ready to roll at a moment's notice.

It's scary to think about the disasters that could strike and leave you stranded for a long period of time without power or water or those that might force you to leave your home and possibly even never return. You can simply hope that a catastrophe never happens and that if one does, you'll figure it out on the fly, or you can take action to have a plan and supplies in place. Wouldn't you feel more comfortable knowing that you have a plan and that you are prepared to take care of your family in the event that a catastrophe does occur? It's simple security. You feel more comfortable having health insurance, car insurance, a home owner's policy right? Emergency preparedness is a form of insurance for you and your family—it covers your practical needs in the case of a disaster. And the beauty is that you get to customize it to your exact needs and wants and can do so with little to no waste of resources. You can make food storage supremely cost efficient.

My experience is that even when people agree that emergency preparedness is important and are comfortable with the idea, they feel overwhelmed and afraid of the process. Let me help you. In the chapters ahead, I'll take you step by step in setting up your plan and your storage so that you can feel safe. Get ready to cross one more concern off the list, so you can spend your energy enjoying life.

STORE THIS ADVICE

Most of the emergency situations outlined above detail disasters. Keep in mind that we also need to be prepared for personal emergencies that can affect our standard of living and safety, such as job loss, disabling accidents, death of the breadwinner, or a serious illness.

PART 1
WHEN THE LIGHTS GO OUT

* * *

HOW TO PREPARE FOR POWER OUTAGES, WATER SHORTAGES, AND FOOD SCARCITY

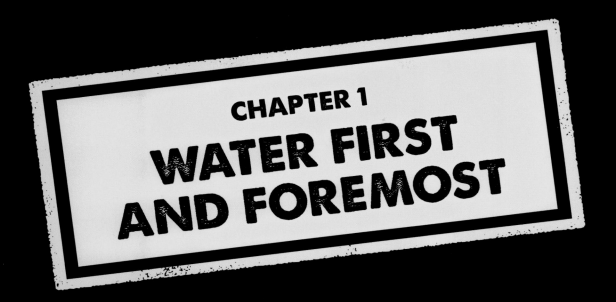

CHAPTER 1
WATER FIRST AND FOREMOST

An aging water pipeline bursts and the homes throughout your community have run dry. You head to the grocery store to find that all of the bottled water is gone, so you drive to the next store and the next—nothing. Damaged pipelines, contaminants, vandalism, drought—any one of these crises can quickly dry up your water supply for days, weeks, maybe longer.

In this chapter, you'll learn why water is the most important part of your preparedness plan. I'll walk you through the different types of water containers that you can use to store water in, how much water your family will need, how to preserve the water safely, and how to purify water for drinking. In an emergency when others are running out of clean drinking water and are in a panic, your family will be calm and comfortable knowing you have plenty of safe water for drinking or staying clean.

Every plan for emergency preparedness must begin with water. You can survive for weeks without food but only days without water. Proper hydration is so important to your body that if you were to allow yourself to become dehydrated in hot and humid conditions, you'd risk getting heatstroke, which can be fatal. Plainly and simply, water is essential to life.

But think about all the other ways it's important to you. From the hour that you get out of bed in the morning until you go to sleep at night, water is part of so many daily rituals. You turn the tap to fill a glass with water and to brush your teeth. You flush the toilet, wash your hands, and scrub your body under a stream of water in the shower or in a tubful of water for a bath. You heat up water on the stove for tea or pour it into your coffeemaker to brew a pot of coffee. You wet a sponge to wipe your counters. You use water to wash your dishes, by hand or in the washer, to do your laundry, to soak your vegetable garden, to prepare meals, and on and on. And, of course, with a simple turn of the tap, you have a nice cool glass of clean water whenever you want one. We use water in so many ways and we have such easy access to it here in the United States, whether from a local municipal supply or a well, that we can easily take it for granted—until it's gone.

WHEN WATER RUNS OUT

You've heard about water running low or drying up in areas that have been suffering from years of drought, like California. At least in these circumstances, residents have some warning as the stream, lake, or reservoir levels begin to drop. More immediate challenges are faced by families whose water supplies become cut off due to water-line breaks, a loss of power at their city's water supply pumps, or contamination from heavy rains, oil spills, sewer-line backups, or industrial waste dumping.

I came across a story not long ago out of Toledo, Ohio. A lake that supplied water to local residents had become overgrown with a type of algae that produces a toxic chemical. The algae had to be killed with a special chemical before the lake water could be made available to residents again. I've read many stories about communities in which people had no access to water in their homes because the city's water supply pumps weren't working.

STORE THIS ADVICE

Find out where the water intake valve is located in your home and be sure to show everyone in your family where it is. Label it in some way, so that it's easy to identify in the future. When local water or sewage lines break, shut the valve off to prevent contaminated water from entering your house.

In any of these events, you could drive to the supermarket in hopes of purchasing cases of bottled water, but if the store shelves are empty, you may find yourself in a situation in which the water you have stored in your home is all that you will have to drink, brush your teeth, and cook your meals for days, possibly weeks, and rationing that water becomes tricky if you don't know when your supply will be restored.

HOW MUCH WATER DO YOU NEED TO STORE?

Your most critical need, of course, is drinking water. Plan to store 1 gallon (3.8 L) per person per day and more if you live in a hot climate. You'll also need some water for cooking and to clean dishes if you're not using paper plates. If you have a supply of freeze-dried or dehydrated foods, you'll want water to rehydrate them. You can eat most freeze-dried food directly from the can or package, but dehydrated products need water to make them consumable and more enjoyable. Then there's personal hygiene—daily teeth brushing and once-a-week hair washing (you can use baby wipes to clean your hands and wash your body). In total—for drinking, cooking, personal hygiene, and washing dishes—plan to store 4 gallons (15.2 L) per person per day.

If you have pets, you'll also need to stock up on drinking water for them. Estimate 1 ounce (30 ml) of water per pound (454 g) of body weight, so if your dog weighs about 40 pounds (18 kg), you'll need 40 ounces (1 L) of water a day (8 cups of water, or 1 quart plus 1 cup).

Should water lines break or power at the water plant go out, you won't have water to flush the toilet. It takes 5 to 12 gallons (19-45 L) of water per day to flush a conventional toilet depending on how many people are using it and how many times it is flushed. If you have access to a nearby pond or lake or you have a pool, you can use that water for flushing, but if that's not the case, I will explain how to create a makeshift dry toilet in chapter 6. Storing enough water for toilet use simply isn't practical.

WATER FORMULA FOR A FAMILY OF FOUR

4 gallons (15 L) per person per day = 16 gallons (61 L) per day

7 days = 7 X 16 gallons (61 L) = 112 gallons (424 L)

14 days = 14 X 16 gallons (61 L) = 224 gallons (848 L)

30 days (1 month) = 454 gallons (1817 L)

Remember, if you have pets, you need to add in their needs for daily drinking water. Figure 1 ounce (30 ml) of water per pound.

A PERFECT EMERGENCY WATER-STORAGE PLAN

I love storing water in WaterBricks because they are easy to handle, and they stack for efficient space-saving storage. I recommend purchasing the 3.5-gallon (13 L) size because it is more cost effective than the smaller containers and much easier to carry than the 5-gallon (19 L) option (I cannot carry a 5-gallon-filled container). Remember to add Water Preserver. One 0.8-ounce (24 ml) bottle treats 55 gallons (208 L) of water, and you'll need to add ½ teaspoon to each 3.5-gallon (13 L) WaterBrick. Here's how to build your emergency water supply using these containers.

FOR A COUPLE

For 3 days

- ☐ 24 gallons (91 L) of water
- ☐ 7 WaterBricks
- ☐ 3 ½ tsp (17 ml) Water Preserver (buy 1 bottle)

For 7 days

- ☐ 56 gallons (212 L) of water
- ☐ 16 WaterBricks
- ☐ 8 tsp (40 ml) Water Preserver (buy 2 bottles)

For 1 month

- ☐ 224 gallons (848 L) of water
- ☐ 64 WaterBricks
- ☐ 32 tsp (160 ml) Water Preserver (buy 2 bottles)

FOR A FAMILY OF THREE

For 3 days

- ☐ 36 gallons (136 L) of water
- ☐ 11 WaterBricks
- ☐ 5 tsp (25 ml) Water Preserver (buy 1 bottle)

For 7 days

- ☐ 84 gallons (318 L) of water
- ☐ 24 WaterBricks
- ☐ 12 tsp (60 ml) Water Preserver (buy 2 bottles)

For 1 month

- ☐ 336 gallons (1,272 L) of water
- ☐ 96 WaterBricks
- ☐ 48 tsp (240 ml) Water Preserver (buy 7 bottles)

FOR A FAMILY OF FOUR

For 3 days

- ☐ 48 gallons (182 L) of water
- ☐ 14 WaterBricks
- ☐ 5 tsp (25 ml) Water Preserver (buy 1 bottle)

For 7 days

- ☐ 112 gallons (424 L) of water
- ☐ 32 WaterBricks
- ☐ 16 tsp (80 ml) Water Preserver (buy 3 bottles)

For 1 month

- ☐ 448 gallons (1,696 L) of water
- ☐ 128 WaterBricks
- ☐ 64 tsp (320 ml) Water Preserver (buy 9 bottles)

FOR A FAMILY OF FIVE

For 3 days

- ☐ 60 gallons (227 L) of water
- ☐ 18 WaterBricks
- ☐ 8 ½ tsp (43 ml) Water Preserver (buy 2 bottles)

For 7 days

- ☐ 140 gallons (530 L) of water
- ☐ 40 WaterBricks
- ☐ 20 tsp (100 ml) Water Preserver (buy 3 bottles)

For 1 month

- ☐ 560 gallons (2,120 L) of water
- ☐ 160 WaterBricks
- ☐ 80 tsp (400 ml) Water Preserver (buy 11 bottles)

CONTAINERS FOR WATER STORAGE

My first priority when I started my journey on food storage was finding a way to store water. I was a young mother, and I filled empty milk jugs with water from the tap. Was it the best? No. Plastic milk containers will eventually leak, but at that time in my life, it was the best affordable option. If you buy beverages in 2-liter bottles, you can also use those to store tap water for drinking if they're properly cleaned. Wash them with dishwashing soap and rinse with water; then mix a teaspoon of bleach in a quart of water and swish it around inside the bottle to sanitize it.

The best containers for storing water are those designed for this purpose. They are made of food-grade, BPA-free, sturdy plastic that won't degrade over time and leak. Many of them are designed to be stackable so that they are easy to store. If your budget doesn't allow you to purchase these types of storage containers, then reuse your milk jugs and other plastic containers to start. As your budget allows—and I talk more about budgeting for emergency preparedness in the next chapter—put aside money for water storage, and as you can, invest in good containers. You will be so thankful that you did.

You have many options for water storage from individual-size packages to 250-gallon (946 L) tanks. What you choose will depend on your personal preference, your living situation, and your budget. Let's take a look at the pros and cons of each.

SMALL CONTAINERS

An emergency or disaster can happen at any time, not just when you're in your own home and staying hydrated can mean surviving or not. Things happen quickly in a disaster and trying to carry very many large containers of water would be impossible, especially if you are alone. You'll want a supply of individual-size packages of water that you can easily grab to take with you in the car or to the office or to pack in your child's schoolbag. If your child is at school when a disaster strikes, you will be comforted to at least know they have some water in their backpack to sustain them until help arrives. It is also important to keep small containers of water in your car, because if something occurs as simple as a traffic jam or as huge as an earthquake, you could easily leave your car and carry a few small containers of water with you to a safer location. And sometimes it's just nice to pop open a single serving of water and drink, no fussing with larger containers and cups or glasses. The disadvantage is that these are not cost effective for storing large volumes of water.

BOTTLED WATER. Perhaps you already purchase bottled water to have on hand in the fridge for yourself or when people come to visit. Just twist off the cap, and it's ready to drink. You can purchase cases of bottled water at your supermarket or online. According to the International Bottled Water Association (bottledwater.org/education/bottled-water-storage) water should be stored at room temperature or cooler and out of direct sunlight. Room temperature is generally considered to be 68° to 77°F (20 to 25°C), so water stored at higher temperatures will not maintain the same quality or taste as bottles stored at lower temperatures. Light and heat can cause chemicals to leach from the plastic into the water, so storing bottled water in a cool, dark place would be the best choice.

The Dasani water company states that its water "will hold its crisp, refreshing taste for up to 12 months. After that, it's best to recycle the old one and start with a fresh, new bottle." Bottled water is meant for a one-time use, and it is recommended that if a bottle is going to be refilled with water, it should be carefully cleaned with soap and warm water and rinsed. Bacterial growth can form in unseen cracks or grooves of plastic, which would then transfer to the water you are drinking. Almost any type of drink container, including coffee mugs, pitchers, or glasses, can contain bacteria if not properly cleaned.

Pros: Clean water in a convenient container.

Cons: Every 6 to 12 months you should replace cases with fresh ones.

Emergency water packets are small and great for a child's 72-hour kit.

EMERGENCY WATER PACKETS. These water packets resemble the juice packets that children love. There are a few different brands. You can purchase them online or at camping supply stores. Check the label to make sure they are United-States-Coast-Guard-approved.

Pros: Simple to stash in your, car, purse, office desk, or your child's school backpack. The packaging is durable yet easy to open, even for a child. Emergency water packets can withstand extreme temperatures so no special storage is required, and their shelf life is five years.

Cons: The drawback is that each packet only holds 4.22 ounces (125 ml). I could drink that much at one meal.

AQUA BLOX EMERGENCY DRINKING WATER. If emergency water packets remind you of juice pouches, these will make you think of juice boxes. They come complete with a straw that you poke through a covered opening. Aqua Blox are also available online or at camping stores.

Pros: These hold more water than the packets—6.75 or 8.45 ounces (200-250 ml). Like the packets, they are United-States-Coast-Guard-approved, have a shelf life of five years, and can withstand extreme temperatures. They're great for 72-hour kits.

Cons: They are crushable, and may leak once crushed, which is why I don't recommend them for a child's backpack.

STORE THIS ADVICE

Be sure to label cases of packaged water or filled containers with the date of storage so that you know when to swap them out for fresh water.

EMERGENCY DRINKING WATER IN A CAN. Yes, you can even buy water in a can, and I really like this option because canned water has an extraordinarily long shelf life and will withstand very cold to very hot temperatures. I put several cases of these in a closet and use them only in an emergency.

Pros: Most have a shelf life of 30 years, but Blue Can's shelf life extends to an amazing 50 years. Blue Can comes in 12-ounce (355 ml) cans (vs. 22 or 24 ounces [651 or 710 ml] for other waters) that are made from 95 percent recycled aluminum.

Cons: Pricey.

Canned water is a handy water storage option, due to its long shelf life.

MEDIUM-SIZE CONTAINERS

Packaged water certainly has its conveniences: it's a perfect grab-and-go option, and because the water is pure and sealed, you don't need to add any preserver. But it's not an efficient or cost-effective way to store large volumes of water. For that purpose, I recommend investing in WaterBricks. These are containers made of food-grade BPA-free plastic that you fill with water, and—here's where the "brick" comes in—they are stackable so they make the most efficient use of your storage space. They come in 1.6- and 3.5-gallon (6-L and 13-L) sizes. The smaller size measures 9 x 9 x 6 inches (23 x 23 x 15cm) and weighs about 13 pounds (208 oz) when filled with water. The larger container measures 9 x 18 x 6 inches (23 x 46 x 15 cm) and tips the scale at about 29 pounds (464 oz). Each has a handle for ease of carrying. I have 16 of the larger WaterBricks under my queen-size bed, which means I have 56 gallons (212 L) of water stored and ready to use when needed. You can purchase a spigot to attach to these containers so that you can set them on the counter and dispense water easily.

Pros: Containers are easier to carry and typically have a handle, plus when filled with water they don't weigh as much as the bigger containers. Even an average teenager could carry a medium-size water container and possibly even two of them depending on the child's size. Another advantage is that most medium-size containers can be stacked to save storage space.

Cons: The medium-size containers are more expensive and would require purchasing 16 (3.5-gallon [13 L]) WaterBricks to equal 56 gallons (212 L) of water (the blue barrels equal 55 gallons [208 L]).

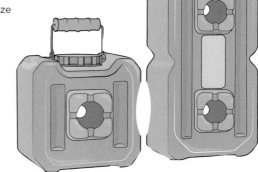

WaterBricks are a great choice when space is limited but you have room under your bed or in a closet to store some water.

BIG AND REALLY BIG WATER STORAGE OPTIONS

How you store water will depend on your home. If you live in an apartment or condo, your most practical option will be to use WaterBricks and some cases of canned emergency water or other packaged water. If you live in a house with a yard, you can consider containers with some significant volume.

WATER-STORAGE BARRELS. You can purchase 55-gallon (208-L) plastic water-storage barrels at your local warehouse store or online for about $50. It's best to place them in a shady area and on a pallet to keep them off the ground. Because summer temperatures can exceed 110 degrees fahrenheit (43°C) in Southern Utah where I live, I use UV covers to protect my 55-gallon (208-L) containers from the heat, and if you're accustomed to winter temperatures below freezing, leave space at the top of the barrel when filling to allow for expansion. You'll need a bung or bucket wrench to tighten the lid of the barrel and a pump to remove water as you need it. Pumps are usually sold alongside the barrels at your local store.

Pros: They are inexpensive and hold 55 gallons (208 L). Most are BPA free (check with the manufacturer before you purchase).

Cons: They are bulky and may be too heavy to store in a small apartment. You need a pump to pump the water out of the barrels, which is hard to control the flow of water and it takes a lot of work (particularly for an elderly person) to manage. The barrels must be placed on 2 x 4 boards (0.6-1.2 M) or another support system other than concrete since the porous nature of the concrete could possibly allow its chemicals to leach into the plastic barrels.

WATER TANKS. The next step—or should I say leap—up in size and cost are water tanks designed for home use. You can purchase 160 or 360-gallon (606-1,362-L) tanks. They are made of BPA-free high-density-polyethylene (durable plastic) and have spigots at ground level and bucket level. Some models have attachments to hook to your water lines so that you can continually rotate the water inside the tank to keep it fresh. My concern though is with possible cross-contamination if the water supply to your home became contaminated by flooding or another unforeseen disaster. Some top suppliers of water storage tanks include Ready Store, Emergency Essentials, and Water Prepared. You can check them out online.

Pros: Some models have 160 gallons (606 L) to 360 gallons (1,363 L) available. Some are stackable

Water storage containers come in various sizes. Cost and available storage space are key factors to consider when making your storage container decisions.

to give you even more gallons available in one location. You can store more water in one location and they typically have two spigots. One spigot or hose bib is just a few inches off the ground to empty the container when you need to rotate the water. The other spigot or hose bib is about 18 inches (46 cm) off the ground and is perfect to fill a bucket. They are BPA free in most cases (check the manufacturer before you purchase).

Cons: They are pricey. Some are as little as $300, but others can cost more than $1,000 each. They weigh a lot and might not be a good fit for every location. They also take up a fair amount of space for those with limited room available.

RAIN BARRELS. These are wonderful if your state allows them—some states don't, so you'll need to check your local laws. The barrel connects to the downspout of your gutter to collect rainwater as it runs down. When you have enough, you can attach a hose to the barrel to water your garden. This water is only safe to drink if properly filtered (see "How to Purify Water"). You can purchase rain barrels at hardware stores and some garden retailers or order them online.

Pros: Rain is free, if we have it, and in some locations rain is abundant.

Cons: The water must be purified before we can drink it. Some states do not allow rainwater collection, so check with your city, county, or state. You will need to make some adjustments to your current rain gutters, if you have rain gutters on your home. If not, you'll have the cost of adding them to direct the rain to the barrel. Rain barrels are fairly expensive, anywhere from $100 to several hundred dollars depending on the make, gallon size, and model.

Be aware that in colder climates the water captured in the rain barrels is subject to freezing. This could cause the rain barrel to burst if too much water is captured. You will need to monitor the water level and drain some out, if necessary, when colder weather sets in. Also, in a rainy season or in the spring when things begin to thaw out and fill the barrels to overflowing levels, you'll need to drain the units. Be sure to have a hose or pump close by to drain the unit before it backs up the drainpipe and causes possible roof or rain gutter damage.

STARTING YOUR WATER STORAGE PLAN

Getting started with buying and storing water follows the same rule of storing food, which you will learn more about in the next chapter. Basically, you should set a goal for how many days you want to be prepared for, check the amounts your family requires, and slowly start buying containers to fit your budget. For instance, most people start with a 55 gallon (208 L) barrel because it is the most economical way to start, but your living conditions (small home or apartment) might not allow a big barrel. So start with small or medium water containers, once again relying on what your budget and space allow. This could mean only buying enough water to last 72 hours and continuing to add more water as you can afford it. Follow the guide for how much water your family would need and start trying to reach that goal. Having 72 hours' worth of water in your closet or under your bed is better than having no water at all. Then store 7 days, then 2 weeks of water, etc. Keep in mind, you need more water than you may realize.

HOW TO PRESERVE DRINKING WATER

Water that you store in containers won't stay fresh without some sort of preservative added to it. I use Water Preserver because it is approved, registered, licensed by the Federal Government and Environmental Protection Agency (EPA), and used by most emergency professionals. And water treated with Water Preserver will last five years before needing to be rotated. Call me lazy, but I don't want to rotate my water every few months because I didn't properly treat it or store it safely. If I can spend a few dollars for an EPA-approved preservative so I only have to rotate my stored water every five years that's what I will do. You can purchase Water Preserver online in 0.8-ounce (24-ml) bottles that treat up to 55 gallons (208 L) of water. Here are suggested amounts to use based on the size of your water storage container:

- ☐ 1.6-gallon (6-L) WaterBrick—¼ teaspoon of Water Preserver
- ☐ 3.5-gallon (13-L) WaterBrick—½ teaspoon of Water Preserver
- ☐ 55-gallon (208-L) barrel—1 bottle of Water Preserver
- ☐ 160-gallon (606-L) High Capacity Water Storage Tank—3 bottles of Water Preserver
- ☐ 250-gallon (946-L) High Capacity Water Storage Tank—4.5 to 5 bottles of Water Preserver
- ☐ Check bottle directions for other size containers

Remember that old idiom—an ounce of prevention (in this case less than an ounce) is worth a pound of cure.

HOW TO PURIFY WATER

What if you're reading this book and you haven't begun to prepare for an emergency when a severe storm strikes and wipes out the local water supply and you have just a few bottles of water in your fridge? Or consider this scenario: you've stored some drinking water, but it appears that you'll run out before clean local municipal water begins flowing again in your home. It's time to think about purifying whatever water you can find—whether that's from a nearby stream, lake, or pond, your water heater or a backyard pool. Remember, water heater water is only safe to drink if you are confident that the supply hasn't been contaminated during the disaster. As for pool water, it may be chlorinated so you can swim in it, but who knows what may have washed into it during the storm or whatever disaster has hit. Also, if the pumps and filtering systems for your pool aren't working, bacteria and algae will start to build up. You don't want to drink any of this water without purifying it. If there is any question about the cleanliness of the water source you are considering, filter first!

A simple solution, which most people have on hand, is bleach. I recommend mixing 8 drops (⅛ teaspoon) of regular bleach (not scented) into each gallon (4 L) of water that you want to make drinkable; let it sit for 30 minutes before you drink it. If you have access to a heat source, you can boil water for one minute—three minutes if you live at a high altitude—to purify it. Boiled water doesn't taste very good, so try aerating it by pouring it back and forth between containers and then allow it to stand for a few hours.

A lot of homes have refrigerator or freestanding water filters that work great to improve the taste of water and remove chlorine, metals, and lead. These types of water filters need to be replaced on a regular basis to avoid bacterial growth. However, most of them do not totally kill bacteria and may actually add bacteria into your water if the filter isn't changed. Therefore, in emergencies when you need to purify water for drinking, I recommend the following filtration systems.

STORE THIS ADVICE

Never drink floodwater, advises the Centers for Disease Control and Prevention. Though you can use a purifier to cleanse water from lakes, streams, or your backyard pool, it may not be able to remove all poisonous contaminants from floodwater.

A FILTRATION SYSTEM IN A BOTTLE

A water bottle purifier is a handy option for your 72-hour kit or camping trip.

I'm a big fan of the Sport Berkey Portable Water Purifier and gave several of them as Christmas gifts to family members one year. It's a sports bottle with a filtration system inside that removes contaminants from water of questionable cleanliness, though I wouldn't recommend using it for water that might have significant bacterial or viral contamination. The beauty of the Sport Berkey is its portability. You can take it on a hike or a camping trip or pack it when traveling in countries where you might be worried about meeting up with Montezuma's revenge. It's great for 72-hour kits (more about those in Chapter 9). You can refill the bottle 640 times using municipal water supplies or 160 times with any other water source before the filter needs to be replaced. It holds approximately 22 ounces (651 ml), is made from BPA-free material, and has a shelf life of 50 years. The Sport Berkey is a fast solution in an unexpected emergency. Consider purchasing one for every member of your family.

PORTABLE FILTERING SYSTEM

A good goal to aim for as you strive for emergency preparedness is to stock up on clean, pure drinking water as well as a filtration system in case your water runs out or to help stretch your stored water. There are several to choose from, but my favorite is the Big Berkey.

Made of stainless steel, it has an upper and lower cylindrical chamber with a diameter of 8.5 inches (22 cm). When fully extended, Big Berkey stands 19.25 inches (49 cm) high, but when you're not using it, the upper chamber nestles into the lower chamber for a height of only 13 inches (33 cm). The Big Berkey is easy to use: place either two or four filters inside the upper chamber and pour your lake or pond water into the top. Gravity pulls the water through the filters and into the lower chamber. When using only two filters, this system purifies about 3.5 gallons (13 L) of water an hour or 84 gallons (318 L) a day. With four filters, the rate increases to 7 gallons (26 L) an hour or 168 gallons (636 L) a day. Using only two filters at a time, you can purify 6,000 gallons (22,712 L) of water before you will need to replace the filters. If you use four filters at a time, you can clean 12,000 gallons (45,425 L) of water before replacements are needed.

For advanced preparedness, large water filters such as the Big Berkey ensure that if you run out of stored drinking water, your family will be able to safely stay hydrated in an emergency.

We've covered a lot of options for water storage. Don't feel like you have to rush out and purchase hundreds of dollars worth of cans, containers, and filtration systems and set up all your storage right away. Think about your options and make a plan for what methods of storage will work best for your family and your home. If you're on a tight budget, try to save $5 a week or a month toward water storage. You'll be surprised at how fast you can save what you need to buy what you really want. In the meantime, start where you can, even if that's cleaning out your milk jugs and filling them with water as I did when I was a young mom.

STORE THIS ADVICE

I've spent this whole chapter discussing why water is such a critical component of your food storage plan. Here's the deal. If you are really serious about taking the steps necessary to be prepared, it's vital that you start all your planning with this question in mind: "What will I do if I don't have access to sufficient water?"

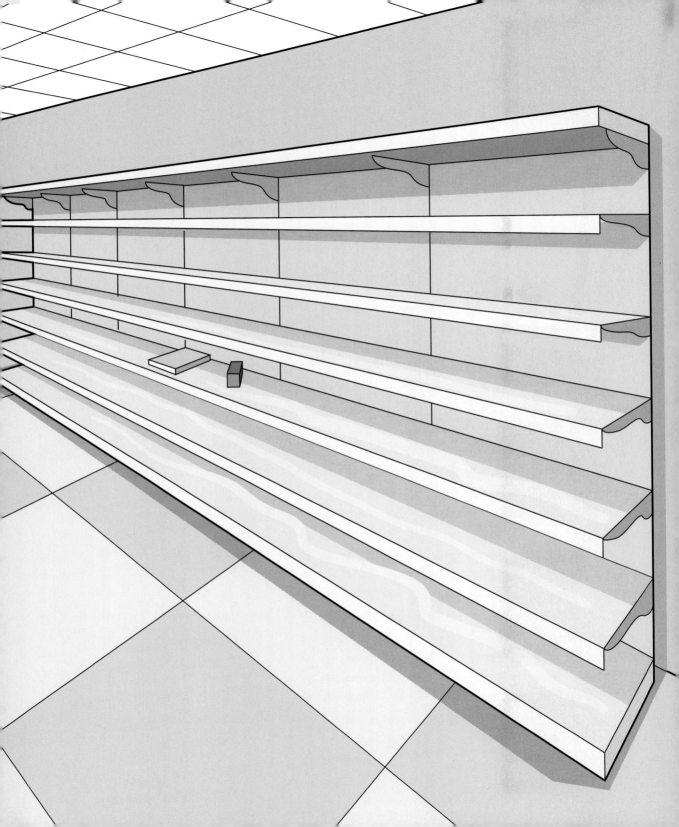

CHAPTER 2
SIMPLE FOOD, SIMPLE STORAGE

Even at the mention of the slightest snowfall, people rush to the grocery store to stock up on milk, bread, and eggs. Now imagine the ice storm barreling into town, pulling down power lines, telephone poles, trees, making roads so slick that tractor trailers jackknife on the highway. Your community becomes immobilized. And the shelves at the market? Bare.

In this chapter, I'll share all of my expertise on food storage—the best types of food, how long they last, how much you'll need, what you can make with them, how to store them, and more. You'll get all the information you need to put together a food storage plan that is customized for you and your family. In an emergency or other difficult situation, you'll be ready to continue serving your family food that is fresh, nutritious, and delicious.

For years I taught food storage and emergency preparedness classes in my neighborhood to help people realize how important it is to be prepared for the unexpected and to help them get prepared. The first thing that comes to mind when we think about food storage is preparing for some major disaster, but the loss of a job or a sudden life-challenging health problem, accident, or injury can also put stress on your family's resources. If you suddenly found yourself unable to collect a paycheck for weeks or possibly months, wouldn't it be comforting to have a stash of food to help you through lean financial times?

I remember one class when someone started laughing about the fact that people might think we are hoarding food if we stock up in preparation for an emergency. Well, I never thought about it that way. I've always stored food for my family, and I feel safer and more comfortable knowing that whatever comes, we will be able to take care of ourselves. Here's the other truth—I don't like grocery shopping. Food storage allows me to make fewer trips to the supermarket.

I stock up on items when they go on sale and only those foods that we eat often. Food storage isn't about buying cases of packaged goods that get stacked on shelves and forgotten until an emergency happens. Everything edible has a shelf life, so you'll want to use and replenish the foods that you purchase to keep them fresh.

Many of the people I've met over the years through my classes and my blog feel a bit overwhelmed and fearful at the thought of food storage, not knowing what to buy or how much. There are many ways to design a food storage plan, and later in this chapter, I will introduce you to the full range of storable foods and guide you through a process of creating the perfect custom plan for your family so that you can create meals much like the ones you serve every day (that's right, you don't have to live on Spam alone when the power goes down). But we each need a place to start when it comes to food storage. So let's begin, not with Spam, but with a variety of canned foods and dried goods that you'll find on your grocery store shelves—before the ice storm hits.

A BASIC FOOD-STORAGE STRATEGY

Here are simple, quick, inexpensive plans to help you stock up on foods for your whole family for three days, a week, or a month. Remember to select the specific fruits, veggies, and meats that you and your family like to eat.

FOR A COUPLE
For 3 days

- ☐ Protein: 6 cans of tuna, chicken, spam, roast beef, or beans
- ☐ Vegetable: 6 cans of green beans, corn, carrots, peas, or other veggies
- ☐ Fruit: 6 cans of applesauce, mandarin oranges, pineapple, or other fruit
- ☐ Grains: 1 (32 oz [907 g]) package of rice
- ☐ Dairy: 1 (25.6 oz [726 g]) package instant milk
- ☐ 1 (32 oz [907 g]) package pancake mix
- ☐ 1 box biscuit mix
- ☐ 1 box cereal
- ☐ 1 (16 oz [454 g]) jar peanut butter
- ☐ 1 (10 oz [283 g]) jar jam
- ☐ 1 (16 oz [454 g]) box crackers
- ☐ 1 (16 oz [454 g]) jar salsa (adds flavor to beans, rice, meats)

For 7 days

- ☐ Protein: 14 cans of tuna, chicken, spam, roast beef, or beans
- ☐ Vegetable: 14 cans of green beans, corn, carrots, peas, or other veggies
- ☐ Fruit: 14 cans of applesauce, mandarin oranges, pineapple, or other fruit
- ☐ Grains: 1 (32 oz [907 g]) package of rice
- ☐ Dairy: 2 (25.6 oz [726 g]) packages instant milk

- ☐ 1 (32 oz [907 g]) package pancake mix
- ☐ 1 box biscuit mix
- ☐ 1 box cereal
- ☐ 1 (16 oz [454 g]) jar peanut butter
- ☐ 1 (10 oz [283 g]) jar jam
- ☐ 1 (16 oz [454 g]) box crackers
- ☐ 1 (16 oz [454 g]) jar salsa (adds flavor to beans, rice, meats)

For 1 month

- ☐ Protein: 60 cans of tuna, chicken, spam, roast beef, or beans
- ☐ Vegetable: 60 cans of green beans, corn, carrots, peas, or other veggies
- ☐ Fruit: 60 cans of applesauce, mandarin oranges, pineapple, or other fruit
- ☐ Grains: 3 (32 oz [907 g]) packages of rice
- ☐ Dairy: 5 (25.6 oz [726 g]) packages instant milk
- ☐ 2 (32 oz [907 g]) packages pancake mix
- ☐ 2 boxes biscuit mix
- ☐ 4 boxes cereal
- ☐ 4 (16 oz [454 g]) jars peanut butter
- ☐ 4 (10 oz [283 g]) jars jam
- ☐ 4 (16 oz [454 g]) boxes crackers
- ☐ 4 (16 oz [454 g]) jars salsa (adds flavor to beans, rice, meats)

(continued)

FOR A FAMILY OF THREE

For 3 days

- ☐ Protein: 9 cans of tuna, chicken, spam, roast beef, or beans
- ☐ Vegetable: 9 cans of green beans, corn, carrots, peas, or other veggies
- ☐ Fruit: 9 cans of applesauce, mandarin oranges, pineapple, or other fruit
- ☐ Grains: 1 (32 oz [907 g]) package of rice
- ☐ Dairy: 1 (25.6 oz [726 g]) package instant milk
- ☐ 1 (32 oz [907 g]) package pancake mix
- ☐ 1 box biscuit mix
- ☐ 1 box cereal
- ☐ 1 (16 oz [454 g]) jar peanut butter
- ☐ 1 (10 oz [283 g]) jar jam
- ☐ 1 (16 oz [454 g]) box crackers
- ☐ 1 (16 oz [454 g]) jar salsa (adds flavor to beans, rice, meats)

For 7 days

- ☐ Protein: 21 cans of tuna, chicken, spam, roast beef, or beans
- ☐ Vegetable: 21 cans of green beans, corn, carrots, peas, or other veggies
- ☐ Fruit: 21 cans of applesauce, mandarin oranges, pineapple, or other fruit
- ☐ Grains: 1 (32 oz [907 g]) package of rice
- ☐ Dairy: 2 (25.6 oz [726 g]) packages instant milk
- ☐ 1 (32 oz [907 g]) package pancake mix
- ☐ 1 box biscuit mix
- ☐ 2 boxes cereal
- ☐ 2 (16 oz [454 g]) jars peanut butter
- ☐ 2 (10 oz [283 g]) jars jam
- ☐ 2 (16 oz [454 g]) boxes crackers
- ☐ 2 (16 oz [454 g]) jars salsa (adds flavor to beans, rice, meats)

For 1 month

- ☐ Protein: 90 cans of tuna, chicken, spam, roast beef, or beans
- ☐ Vegetable: 90 cans of green beans, corn, carrots, peas, or other veggies
- ☐ Fruit: 90 cans of applesauce, mandarin oranges, pineapple, or other fruit
- ☐ Grains: 5 (32 oz [907 g]) packages of rice
- ☐ Dairy: 9 (25.6 oz [726 g]) packages instant milk
- ☐ 3 boxes pancake mix
- ☐ 2 boxes biscuit mix
- ☐ 6 boxes cereal
- ☐ 6 (16 oz [454 g]) jars peanut butter
- ☐ 6 (10 oz [283 g]) jars jam
- ☐ 4 (16 oz [454 g]) boxes crackers
- ☐ 6 (16 oz [454 g]) jars salsa (adds flavor to beans, rice, meats)

FOR A FAMILY OF FOUR

For 3 days

- ☐ Protein: 12 cans of tuna, chicken, spam, roast beef, or beans
- ☐ Vegetable: 12 cans of green beans, corn, carrots, peas, or other veggies
- ☐ Fruit: 12 cans of applesauce, mandarin oranges, pineapple, or other fruit
- ☐ Grains: 1 (32 oz [907 g]) package of rice
- ☐ Dairy: 1 (25.6 oz [726 g]) package instant milk
- ☐ 1 (32 oz [907 g]) package pancake mix
- ☐ 1 box biscuit mix
- ☐ 1 box cereal
- ☐ 1 (16 oz [454 g]) jar peanut butter
- ☐ 1 (10 oz [283 g]) jar jam
- ☐ 1 (16 oz [454 g]) box crackers
- ☐ 1 (16 oz [454 g]) jar salsa (adds flavor to beans, rice, meats)

For 7 days

☐ Protein: 28 cans of tuna, chicken, spam, roast beef, or beans

☐ Vegetable: 28 cans of green beans, corn, carrots, peas, or other veggies

☐ Fruit: 28 cans of applesauce, mandarin oranges, pineapple, or other fruit

☐ Grains: 2 (32 oz [907 g]) packages of rice

☐ Dairy: 3 (25.6 oz [726 g]) packages instant milk

☐ 1 (32 oz [907 g]) package pancake mix

☐ 1 box biscuit mix

☐ 2 boxes cereal

☐ 2 (16 oz [454 g]) jars peanut butter

☐ 2 (10 oz [283 g]) jars jam

☐ 2 (16 oz [454 g]) boxes crackers

☐ 2 (16 oz [454 g]) jars salsa (adds flavor to beans, rice, meats)

For 1 month

☐ Protein: 120 cans of tuna, chicken, spam, roast beef, or beans

☐ Vegetable: 120 cans of green beans, corn, carrots, peas, or other veggies

☐ Fruit: 120 cans of applesauce, mandarin oranges, pineapple, or other fruit

☐ Grains: 6 (32 oz [907 g]) packages of rice

☐ Dairy: 12 (25.6 oz [726 g]) packages instant milk

☐ 6 (32 oz [907 g]) packages pancake mix

☐ 3 boxes biscuit mix

☐ 6 boxes cereal

☐ 9 (16 oz [454 g]) jars peanut butter

☐ 9 (10 oz [283 g]) jars jam

☐ 5 (16 oz [454 g]) boxes crackers

☐ 8 (16 oz [454 g]) jars salsa (adds flavor to beans, rice, meats)

FOR A FAMILY OF FIVE

For 3 days

☐ Protein: 15 cans of tuna, chicken, spam, roast beef, or beans

☐ Vegetable: 15 cans of green beans, corn, carrots, peas, or other veggies

☐ Fruit: 15 cans of applesauce, mandarin oranges, pineapple, or other fruit

☐ Grains: 1 (32 oz [907 g]) package of rice

☐ Dairy: 2 (25.6 oz [726 g]) packages instant milk

☐ 1 (32 oz [907 g]) package pancake mix

☐ 1 box biscuit mix

☐ 1 box cereal

☐ 1 (16 oz [454 g]) jar peanut butter

☐ 1 (10 oz [283 g]) jar jam

☐ 1 (16 oz [454 g]) box crackers

☐ 1 (16 oz [454 g]) jar salsa (adds flavor to beans, rice, meats)

For 7 days

☐ Protein: 35 cans of tuna, chicken, spam, roast beef, or beans

☐ Vegetable: 35 cans of green beans, corn, carrots, peas, or other veggies

☐ Fruit: 35 cans of applesauce, mandarin oranges, pineapple, or other fruit

☐ Grains: 2 (32 oz [907 g]) packages of rice

☐ Dairy: 7 (25.6 oz [726 g]) packages instant milk

☐ 2 (32 oz [907 g]) packages pancake mix

☐ 2 boxes biscuit mix

☐ 3 boxes cereal

☐ 2 (16 oz [454 g]) jars peanut butter

☐ 2 (10 oz [283 g]) jars jam

☐ 2 (16 oz [454 g]) boxes crackers

☐ 2 (16 oz [454 g]) jars salsa (adds flavor to beans, rice, meats)

(continued)

For 1 month

- ☐ Protein: 150 cans of tuna, chicken, spam, roast beef, or beans
- ☐ Vegetable: 150 cans of green beans, corn, carrots, peas, or other veggies
- ☐ Fruit: 150 cans of applesauce, mandarin oranges, pineapple, or other fruit
- ☐ Grains: 8 (32 oz [907 g]) packages of rice
- ☐ Dairy: 14 (25.6 oz [726 g]) packages instant milk
- ☐ 8 (32 oz [907 g]) packages pancake mix
- ☐ 4 boxes biscuit mix
- ☐ 10 boxes cereal
- ☐ 11 (16 oz [454 g]) jars peanut butter
- ☐ 11 (10 oz [283 g]) jars jam
- ☐ 5 (16 oz [454 g]) boxes crackers
- ☐ 11 (16 oz [454 g]) jars salsa (adds flavor to beans, rice, meats)

See the section on "What to Cook" (page 56) for a whole list of foods that can be cooked with my food storage items. Also keep in mind that most of the items in this storage plan you can eat right out of the can.

EXPANDING YOUR FOOD STORAGE HORIZONS

Canned goods are a convenient and comfortable option, but dehydrated and freeze-dried foods have certain advantages for storage that you might want to consider.

Most people have no experience with dehydrated or freeze-dried food, and I understand how mysterious these products may seem when we're accustomed to eating and cooking with canned or fresh whole fruits and vegetables. I'm going to help take away the mystery and show you how these foods can be part of your emergency stores. Several factors come into play as you consider your ideal food plan, including cost, convenience, shelf life, and the amount of storage space you have. I will guide you in your personal plan for choosing what to store, how much to store, and where to store it. Let me first introduce you to the variety of storable-food options available to you, beginning with our old standby.

CANNED FOODS

The first, most familiar, and easiest place to start with food storage is canned foods. You likely already buy certain canned goods—canned tomatoes, soups, tuna fish, beans perhaps. As you start developing your food storage plan, you'll want to consider what other foods you would eat out of a can. Perhaps you rarely if ever buy canned green beans, peaches, or even something like SpaghettiOs, but think about how you might expand your range of canned foods for storage. If canned peas usually do not have a place on your pantry shelves, ask yourself if you would be happy to eat them during a food shortage.

Pros: You have an abundance of foods to choose from: vegetables, fruits, and beans, of course, but also canned meats like tuna, chicken, and ham, and even desserts like puddings. You can purchase in bulk, making this an inexpensive food storage option.

Cons: Canned foods take up more storage space than dehydrated or freeze-dried foods and are heavier than those two options if you plan to pack food for a 72-hour kit or bug-out bag. Dehydrated and freeze-dried foods have a longer shelf life.

Shelf life: Commercially canned foods have a shelf life of two to five years from the date of manufacture and should have an expiration date printed on the can.

HOME-CANNED FOODS

If you have your own garden or can purchase fresh produce from a Community Supported Agriculture (CSA) farm or local farmer's market, you might want to consider canning your own fruits and vegetables. My mother taught me how to can foods, and I taught my daughters. We worked together, the girls separating the apricots or peaches from their pits. It was one of the ways we connected as a family, and my daughters, who are grown now, still sometimes talk about their memories of helping me can foods. I've canned just about everything, including peaches, pears, apples, tomatoes, salsa, and marinara sauce. It's important to use proper canning practices to prevent bacteria from growing inside, which could cause food poisoning. To learn how to can foods properly and safely, visit the following website links:

freshpreserving.com/getting-started (This is the Ball canning method—my favorite!)
extension.usu.edu/canning
nchfp.uga.edu/publications/publications_usda.html

Pros: Because you can from the garden at the peak of freshness, home-canned fruits and vegetables will taste better than commercially canned foods, and you feel a certain satisfaction eating your own food.

Cons: It's a lot of work, but it's very gratifying to look at all the jars of foods you've canned. Like commercially canned foods, these will take up more storage space than dehydrated or freeze-dried products.

Shelf life: Home-canned foods are good for a year unopened.

STORE THIS ADVICE

☐ You can use the excess liquid in canned foods to reconstitute freeze-dried foods.

☐ It is essential that you have a good can opener or even two in case you misplace one or want to lend one to a neighbor in need.

HOME GROWN

My husband and I have always had a garden, and I've canned a huge variety of fruits and vegetables. I love digging in the dirt, putting in onion seeds, and watching them grow. I can grow spinach year round. My basil will get 3 feet (1 M) tall and I can simply go out and clip leaves whenever I need some.

If you have access to a small plot of land, consider putting in a garden. It's an adventure. Involve your younger children. They may not be crazy about pulling weeds, but they will love watching the plants grow to maturity, and they'll have fun harvesting the ripe fruits and vegetables. You don't need a lot of land. My husband and I put in some raised beds that are 4 feet by 4 feet (1.2 by 1.2 M). We built them high enough for me to work the soil and plants without kneeling down or having to bend over very much.

If you don't have a yard, consider organizing a neighborhood garden. Some towns have taken vacant lots and turned them into community gardens where neighbors share in the labor of planting and tending the garden, and then in the harvest. There's nothing like a just-picked ripe tomato or a peach plucked from the tree in your backyard.

DEHYDRATED FOODS

For centuries humans have been preparing food for long-term storage. One of the most common ways of preserving meat was to salt it so it didn't spoil and then hang it to dry. People discovered that drying meat and other foods reduced their weight and volume. Today, dehydrating foods—which is simply a process for removing water—has become modernized and commercialized so that you don't have to do it yourself, though you could if you had a dehydrator.

I have dehydrated just about every fruit or vegetable you can imagine, and I still do it from time to time. Recently I was able to buy a large container of spinach—more spinach than my husband and I could eat before it would spoil—so I dehydrated the bulk of it, filling a number of small canning jars with the dry leaves. I was amazed to see how little space the spinach required once it was dried. Now each day I take out a jar and use the spinach in my smoothies for the flavor and nutrients it adds. Although not identified as such, many of the foods we eat every day are actually dehydrated—cereal, pasta, beans, and spices. You can purchase powdered milk, eggs, butter, soups, marinara sauces, and mixes for baked goods. Needless to say, they aren't very edible without adding liquid and rehydrating them. Generally, dehydrated foods are best added to soups, stews, or casseroles where they plump up with liquid as they cook.

Pros: Efficient for storage since they are light and take up less space than canned goods. Less expensive than freeze-dried foods.

Cons: Pricier than canned goods. They require liquid to make them palatable. If you hope to dehydrate foods on your own for long-term storage, know that it's a lot of work—you'll need not only to dehydrate the food, you'll need to package it for long-term storage.

Shelf life: Five to eight years. If there's not an expiration date on the package, label it with the date of purchase and use and replenish these foods before they expire. Once opened, the shelf life drops to 6 months up to a year.

FREEZE-DRIED FOOD

Foods that are freeze-dried go through a much more involved process than their dehydrated cousins. The fruit, vegetable, or meat is first flash frozen and then exposed to low heat in a vacuum chamber. The finished product is superior to dehydrated foods in flavor and nutritional content. In most cases you can eat the food directly out of the package. When I taught classes, I served samples of every freeze-dried fruit or vegetable I could find. Try corn, green beans, and peas right out of the can. The strawberries, pineapple, bananas, and apples are delicious as well and make super snacks.

I cook with freeze-dried meats and cheeses as well. I have cheddar, Colby, mozzarella and Monterey Jack in storage right now, and I find I no longer throw out moldy cheese because of the infrequency with which my husband and I eat cheese. I've used freeze-dried cheese and meats in chicken salad, tacos, lasagna, chicken enchiladas, and other meals, and they taste just as good as the same meals made with fresh ingredients.

Pros: Long shelf life. Don't require lots of storage room. Convenient. The freeze-drying process retains most of the nutrient value and flavor. They require less water and cook faster than dehydrated foods, and you can eat them right out of the package. They tend to rehydrate quickly and taste pretty close to their freshly picked original flavor and texture. Studies have shown that the nutrition content of freeze-dried foods is higher than most dehydrated foods.

Cons: Pricey. I justify the added cost because I can cook with freeze-dried foods every day and make fewer trips to the grocery store. I also like the idea that I can eat the fruits and vegetables right out of the container for a quick and healthy snack.

Shelf life: Typically 20 years unopened and about 2 years after opening. Check the package because shelf life varies depending on the manufacturer and the environment in which you store it—most companies recommend storing freeze-dried foods at temperatures between 60 and 70°F (16 and 21°C) for maximum longevity.

STORE THIS ADVICE

When shopping for dehydrated and freeze-dried foods, a D on the package label indicates dehydrated; FD means freeze-dried. Not all packages are labeled, however, so ask the salesperson for help if you don't see a mark.

WHAT IS A #10 CAN?

This common container for foods sold for food storage measures 7 inches (18 cm) high and 6 ¼ inches (16 cm) in diameter. It's the size of a typical can of coffee that you see on supermarket shelves and comes with a plastic lid to help keep food fresh after opening.

SHOPPING FOR DEHYDRATED AND FREEZE-DRIED FOODS

Typically, you won't find dehydrated or freeze-dried foods in your grocery store. Some brands are sold in brick-and-mortar retail stores, but all of them are available online where you can compare their features and prices. Here are several brands that I like.

LONG-TERM SHELF LIFE

Augason Farms: augasonfarms.com
You can find these at Walmart, and some items are available on Amazon.com.

Emergency Essentials: beprepared.com (look under food storage)
This Utah-based company has a few retail stores in its home state.

Honeyville: honeyville.com
This brand operates a few brick-and-mortar stores in the West, and some items are available on Amazon.com.

Mountain House: mountainhouse.com
Mountain House foods are also sold at Emergency Essentials retail stores and on Amazon.com.

Thrive Life: thrivelife.com
Only available online.

SHORT-TERM SHELF LIFE

North Bay Trading Company: northbaytrading.com

North Bay offers foods in smaller packages and they have some organic options.
Only available online.

5 SIMPLE STEPS TO FOOD STORAGE

Purchasing and storing food for emergencies can seem an overwhelming task and a great financial burden, but if you take it in steps over time, it's easy—really. You don't need to have everything in place tomorrow, but you can start today. By taking a planned, thoughtful, step-by-step approach to food storage, you can do this with ease and efficiency and without wasting time, money, or food.

STEP 1: MAKE A LIST OF WHAT YOU LIKE

You may think you already know what you like, but remember, the foods you store need to have a long shelf life, so your focus should be on canned, dehydrated, and freeze-dried foods. Start by looking in your cupboard and making a list of what you see there. Think about what you know gets eaten without complaints. The next time you go to the grocery store, walk the aisles slowly and take a good look at the canned foods. Which ones do you usually purchase? Which ones would you want to eat? This is especially important if you and your family eat few canned foods. You need to determine what you will eat out of a can. If you always buy peas in the freezer section, will you and your family be okay eating canned peas? I know people say when you're hungry you'll eat anything, but when you're planning for food storage why buy something you don't like? Emergency situations are tough enough without having to eat something you hate just to survive. While you're perusing the shelves at your supermarket, pick up a can or two of something you know everyone likes, and when you get home put it in a box designated for storage. You see? You're already on your way.

Consider also purchasing a can of peas or whatever vegetable or fruit you usually eat fresh and try it out at home with your family. If everyone likes it, add it to your list. Take the same approach with dehydrated or freeze-dried foods—try before you buy. Purchase small packages that you and your family can sample or try in your cooking. When a food gets a thumbs-up, make a note. They say that variety is the spice of life. Be adventuresome and taste fruits, vegetables, grains, and proteins that you've never eaten before. I have a few suggestions, which I'll share a little later in this chapter.

Creating your food storage list should involve the whole family. Ask everyone to participate and tell you what he or she likes or would like to try. As with buying and storing the food itself, this list won't be completed in a day. Add to it over time as your family tries new foods, and in the meantime, pick up what you do like—a can at a time.

STEP 2: BUY A CAN (OR TWO) AT A TIME

The question I'm always asked when it comes to food storage is, "Where do I start?" My standard reply is, "one can at a time." If over the past year you had purchased $5, $10, or $25 in food storage items each month, imagine what you'd have on your shelves right now. Don't think you have to run up your credit card to stock up on a month's worth of food and water by the weekend. That kind of thinking keeps a lot of people from starting a food storage plan. Each time you shop, pick up one or two food items to put in storage based on the meal plans you've created and the list of foods you and your family love. You won't even notice the few extra dollars spent, and you'll feel really good that you are working to achieve your food storage goal.

Set a target of getting three days' worth of extra food and water for your family using the Basic Food-Storage Strategy included earlier in this chapter. Use the list you made in Step 1 to start stocking items that your family likes and eats regularly. After you have three days' worth of food stored, continue to add to your stores until you have a week's supply that would adequately and comfortably feed you and your family. Eventually, you can work up to a month's or even a year's supply if that's your long-term plan.

Watch for coupons and look for opportunities to buy in bulk to take advantage of the savings. Talk with family, friends, and neighbors to see if they would be interested in going in on a case of food or water. Perhaps they are working on their own emergency-preparedness plan and would welcome an opportunity to partner with you in ordering freeze-dried or dehydrated foods in bulk.

Start with just one can, build gradually, and look for ways to save money on your purchases. With this approach you'll find that food storage is simple, and as you watch your supply grow, you'll love the feeling it gives you to know you can feed your family for a month or more if a disaster occurs.

STEP 3: PLAN FOR THE BASICS

Understanding what basic foods are needed for your storage plan will provide that extra level of comfort knowing you can properly feed your family and survive.

You will want to include some staples for cooking and baking. If a disaster damages power and gas lines, and you are not able to use your stove or oven, there are other ways to cook food, which I'll review in the next chapter. Take a look at my list of recommended cooking basics.

BAKING SODA AND BAKING POWDER. Both are used to make cakes, muffins, or other delicious bakery items rise. Baking soda is said to have a long shelf life, but you'll want to check with the manufacturer for details and be sure to rotate it often.

BROTH OR BOUILLON. I stock chicken, beef, and ham bouillon in my pantry. Bouillon comes in cubes, liquid, or paste and will need to be reconstituted with water in order to use. The paste needs to be refrigerated after opening, so for long-term storage go with cubes or liquid. My favorite bouillon is Better Than Bouillon, and you can usually find it in the soup aisle in most grocery stores. Ready-to-use broth can be purchased in cans or cartons. The shelf life is typically one to two years.

BUTTER. For food storage your choices here are powdered or canned butter. Now, I have to tell you that I've tried just about every brand of powdered butter available, and I do not care for any of them. Powdered butter would probably be fine for cookies or other recipes, but I wouldn't spread it on my toast. I do like the canned butter made by Red Feather. If you want to try some powdered butter, purchase just one can and then if you like it, you can buy a case. The shelf life of powdered butter is about three to five years. Red Feather says their butter lasts two to five years, although I have talked to people who opened a can after 20 years and said the butter was delicious.

CORNMEAL. I buy regular cornmeal for corn bread, and I buy the brand MASECA instant corn masa flour to make corn tortillas. I store both of these in the freezer to prolong their shelf life. The typical shelf life for cornmeal is five years in an unopened commercially processed can, not a box.

CORNSTARCH. This is a must-have for thickening gravies and puddings. Cornstarch can be kept indefinitely if kept dry.

EGGS. You can purchase eggs to store in many forms: powdered, precooked or freeze-dried scrambled eggs, scrambled egg mix, whole egg powder, and egg white powder. Shelf life depends on the specific product and manufacturer. Be sure to check expiration dates.

FLOUR. A bag of white flour from the supermarket has a shelf life of 12 to 18 months. I only store the amount of white flour that I will use within 12 months. I like to buy #10 cans of white all-purpose flour with a shelf life of five years if unopened (see "White Flour Market" for online suppliers of white flour). Once whole-wheat grain is ground into flour it goes rancid very quickly and only has a shelf life of about one month, unless it is stored in the freezer, which extends its life to about six months. Every day that freshly ground flour is in your pantry or on your counter it is losing nutrients. I grind mine and immediately place it in the freezer for a maximum of one month if I'm not using it that day.

WHITE FLOUR MARKET

You can buy white flour at most grocery stores or consider these online shops.

Honeyville (honeyville.com): Their Fantastic Bread Flour comes in sealed 50-pound (22-kg) bags and has a shelf life of one year, unopened or opened, when stored in a cool dry place.

Thrive Life (thrivelife.com): Thrive's all-purpose unbleached white flour comes in #10 cans and can be stored for five years unopened under optimal conditions (70°F [21°C] at most). Once you open it, plan to use it within the year.

LINDA'S WHITE BREAD

Here's the deal, if you can make bread, you can survive by eating and bartering with it. I can picture people lining up to trade something for a fresh loaf of homemade bread. Most everyone likes bread, even though some people are shying away from eating very much due to health issues. With bread you open up a wide variety of meal options and combinations with other food products. And on top of that, you learn a valuable skill in preparing a staple food from scratch that you can make regularly with your family.

I use this recipe to make bread, rolls, bread sticks, and cinnamon rolls.

BASIC BREAD RECIPE YIELD: 3 LOAVES

2 cups (473 ml) warm milk

½ cup (118 ml) warm water

4 tsp (110 g) SAF Instant Yeast

¼ cup (59 ml) oil

1 cup (200 g) sugar

1 ½ tsp (12 g) salt

4 tsp (15 g) dough enhancer (optional)

2 eggs, slightly beaten

6-7 cups (720-840 g) white flour

Preheat oven to 350°F (177°C).

In a large bowl mix all the ingredients except the flour. Add flour until the dough pulls away from the sides of the bowl.

Divide the dough out into three equal portions, then roll into rectangles, approximately 6 x 9 inches (15 x 23 cm), and fold into thirds. Place in greased 1-pound (16-oz) loaf pans, cover with plastic wrap, and let rise until double the original size.

Bake for 27 to 30 minutes or until golden brown.

A note on rising: Let the dough rise until double the original size, which takes about 1-2 hours depending on the temperature in the room. It will rise much faster if the room is not cold. If you put two fingers in the dough and it leaves an imprint, the dough is ready to bake.

You can vary the recipe to make bread sticks or cinnamon rolls. Simply follow the instructions above to make the dough, then roll it and bake it according to the recipe on the next page.

BREAD STICKS

Preheat oven to 350°F (177°C).

Roll dough out into a rectangle approximately 12 x 18 inches (30 x 46 cm) and cut in strips. Dip each strip in melted butter and place on a baking sheet, cover with plastic wrap, and let rise until double the original size.

Remove the plastic wrap and bake for 15 to 20 minutes, depending on the size of the bread sticks, until light golden brown.

CINNAMON ROLLS

Preheat oven to 350°F (177°C).

Roll the dough out into a rectangle approximately 12 x 18 inches (30 x 46 cm). Spread the dough with butter and sprinkle with cinnamon and brown sugar. Roll up and cut into slices 2 inches (5 cm) thick. Place on greased cookie sheet, cover with greased plastic wrap, and let rise until double the original size.

Remove the plastic wrap and bake for 15 to 20 minutes until light golden brown. Be careful not to overbake. Makes 12 to 15 cinnamon rolls.

CREAM CHEESE FROSTING

1 cube softened butter

1 (8 oz [227 g]) package of cream cheese, softened

3 ½ cups (700 g) powdered sugar

2 tsp (10 ml) vanilla

Place all the ingredients in a bowl and beat with a mixer until smooth. Use it to frost cinnamon rolls, warm or cold.

Notes: I suggest storing a few cans of powdered eggs and instant milk so you can substitute those for fresh products and still make bread. If you can't heat the milk to make it warm it will just take a bit longer for your bread to rise. Even if the bread doesn't rise it will be edible, but probably not as fluffy as the regular bread you make or buy at the grocery store.

I suggest in the book a number of times that heating meals by using a butane stove is a cost-effective option and one that could be used to heat the milk. Baking the bread without gas or water could be a challenge, but I've used a sun oven to bake my bread and it comes out great.

I only use SAF Instant Yeast. It is the only one I trust to make any of my breads. The dough enhancer I prefer is made by L'Equip. Though it is optional, it makes the bread, rolls, and bread sticks light and fluffy. You can buy dough enhancer online (Amazon) and it's available at most grocery stores in the baking aisle.

MILK. You have a few choices when it comes to storing milk: instant milk powder, non-instant milk powder, evaporated, and sweetened condensed. A different process is used to make the two different powdered milks. Instant is better for drinking and non-instant is intended primarily for cooking and baking. Both have a shelf life of 25 years unopened and about two years after opening. You can also buy buttermilk in powdered form, and it has a shelf life of three to five years unopened, six months after opening. Evaporated milk and sweetened condensed milk come in cans and have a shelf life of about six months; be sure to check expiration dates and rotate your stash so it doesn't spoil.

OATS. Steel-cut, regular, or quick oats—most will last for 2 to 3 years if stored in a cool, dry place. Keep an eye on the expiration date. When in doubt, throw it out.

OILS (VEGETABLE, OLIVE, COCONUT, AND CANOLA) AND SHORTENING. These all generally have a shelf life of only one to two years and can go rancid quite quickly. Coconut oil lasts longer than most oils, but it will depend on the storage temperature. Keep all oils and shortenings in a properly sealed container and store in a cool, dark place. I prefer to store powdered shortening for emergencies because it has a shelf life of three to five years.

SALT. Regular table salt, coarse salt, or sea salt are important for enhancing the flavor of foods. Salt never spoils or goes bad, but moisture can cause it to clump. You may need to break it up if it's been in storage for a long period.

SEASONINGS. Chili powder, dry mustard, oregano, onion powder, garlic powder, cayenne pepper, basil, parsley flakes, red pepper flakes, and pepper are some of the spices you'll want to have on hand. Check your cupboard to see what spices you and your family use most often, and watch for sales at your supermarket since some spices can prove to be a little pricey. I've had spices in my cupboard that were over a year old, but the flavor is noticeably weaker than those in fresh jars. Check expiration dates and rotate seasonings to keep the flavors at their peak.

SOUP BASE. You should be able to buy a soup base in #10 cans at your local grocery store. Simply add water, boil, then add vegetables or meat as desired and cook until done—easy, right? And tasty. You can also make a thin white sauce to serve over foods or a cream-soup base by adding powdered butter, water, milk, and flour. Check expiration dates because they vary by brand.

SUGAR AND OTHER SWEETENERS. Granulated white sugar, powdered sugar, and brown sugar are most commonly used in baking and to sweeten beverages and foods, and they can last indefinitely. Sugar doesn't spoil because it doesn't support bacterial growth, however, it may clump or harden. You can soften brown sugar with a piece of fresh bread thrown in the bag. White sugar can be broken with a strong utensil or hammer.

HONEY. Regular liquid honey comes in various flavors depending on the most prominent plants the bees are using to gather nectar, with clover being one of the most common. It can be stored indefinitely but may harden. You can liquefy it by heating it in the microwave, though the manufacturers of Cox's Honey in Shelley, Idaho, say this form of high-temperature heat can destroy nutrients. A better way to soften the honey is by placing it in a pan of water over heat. You can also store honey crystals or honey powder but their shelf life may be shorter. Check with the manufacturer.

I recommend Cox's Honey, because it is raw, unfiltered, pure honey. If you happen to be visiting Shelley, Idaho, you can purchase honey at their store, but most of us will need to order it from their website, coxshoney.com. The process of filtering and heating honey removes most of the pollen and nutrients. Unfiltered honey, which retains pollen, contains more nutrients and therefore is more healthful. To learn more, visit the Food Safety News website.

MAPLE SYRUP. You have lots of choices of brands and types—some are pure maple syrup, others are corn syrup with a maple flavoring. Either lasts less than a year.

ARTIFICIAL SWEETENERS AND STEVIA. If you have diabetes and use artificial sweetener, sucralose (brand name Splenda), which is made from sugar molecules is shelf stable and has no expiration date. If your preference is for Stevia, which is a sweetener derived from an herb, it will last two to three years in a cool place, unopened. If opened, the shelf life is only three to six months, so for storage, you might consider getting boxes of the individual packets of Stevia.

SUPPLEMENTS. Okay, technically not a food, but if you take any supplements regularly for your health— calcium, vitamin D, fish oil, even a multivitamin—keep extra bottles in storage based on expiration dates and your supplement usage.

VANILLA EXTRACT OR VANILLA BEANS. This is a must-have if you plan to do any baking. Vanilla extract has a shelf life of about three years. The beans can be kept indefinitely if stored in a cool, dry, dark place.

VINEGAR. An ingredient in salad dressings and marinades, you can also mix it with water to use for cleaning. The acidity of vinegar helps to preserve it, giving it an indefinite shelf life.

WATER. You'll need water to drink and to prepare almost every meal. Learn all about how to store water in Chapter 1.

WHEAT. You can grind wheat into flour to be used in breads, cakes, and other baked goods, or you can soak it and cook it to make cereal. You can sprout it and add it to salads or use it to make wheatgrass drinks. Wheat can be stored indefinitely but is best if rotated every five years. I prefer hard white wheat. Its flavor is not as strong as the hard red wheat, which is used to make the whole-wheat flour you find in grocery stores. I've been making homemade bread for years (see "Linda's Whole-Wheat Bread," on the next page), and I grind my wheat and store it in the freezer for one month or so. If you leave freshly ground flour in your pantry it will become rancid very quickly.

THE GRAIN MAKER

There are many hand-crank grain mills available in varying prices. I opted to buy the GrainMaker made in Stevenson, Montana. These mills are handcrafted here in the United States. They are extremely sturdy and can grind many grains and make several types of cereal. You simply adjust the mill to grind the consistency you desire. And I love that it's an heirloom piece that I can hand down to my kids.

LINDA'S WHOLE-WHEAT BREAD

My whole-wheat bread recipe is included for those looking for a healthier bread to eat by grinding your own wheat. I purchase hard white whole wheat because the flavor is not as strong as the kind our grandmothers used to make. Most people used to buy hard red wheat 30-40 years ago. If you remember those heavy brick type loaves of bread you will love this recipe because it's totally different but still easy. If your ingredients are fresh, anyone can make bread—I promise. I store my yeast, dough enhancer, and wheat gluten in the freezer to keep them fresh, and I keep small containers in my refrigerator for regular use.

This recipe, like my white bread recipe, can be baked and bartered for almost anything after a disaster. If you can make bread you can survive with water.

YIELD: 4 (4 X 8-IN [10 X 20 CM]) LOAVES

3 cups (711 ml) warm water

⅓ cup (79 ml) olive oil

½ cup (118 ml) honey

1 tbsp (8 g) dough enhancer (optional)

1 tbsp (8 g) wheat gluten (optional)

1 tbsp (20 g) salt

1 tbsp (8 g) dry instant or powdered milk

1 tbsp (8 g) SAF Instant Yeast

1 tbsp (15 ml) lemon juice

7-7 ½ cups (840-900 g) whole-wheat flour

Put the warm water in a large bowl or a bread mixer. Add the rest of the ingredients except 3 ½ cups (60 g) of the flour. Mix for about 1 minute in the mixer or by hand. Add the other 3 ½ cups (60 g) of flour and continue mixing for 10 minutes with a bread mixer or knead by hand for about 20 minutes. Add more flour as needed until the dough pulls away from the sides of the bowl. Let the bread rise for about an hour and then punch it down to remove the air. Form into four loaves and place in greased 4 x 8-inch (10 x 20 cm) loaf pans. Cover with greased plastic wrap and let rise for one to two hours until your finger makes a slight indentation in the dough. Bake at 350°F (177°C) for 30 minutes or until the tops are a golden brown.

Notes: If you ever have tasted whole-wheat bread "bricks" and do not care for the heavy consistency, you will want to use the dough enhancer and wheat gluten. Though they are optional, I highly recommend them. They improve the texture and make the bread light and fluffy.

This recipe makes four loaves, but can easily be doubled for larger families.

YEAST. SAF Instant Yeast comes in a one-pound (454-g) vacuum-sealed package and has a shelf life of five years if unopened. Once opened, the shelf life is six months if stored in an airtight container in a cupboard or pantry or a year or longer if stored in the freezer. I store the bulk of my SAF Instant Yeast in the freezer and put a small amount that I'll use every other week in a container that I store in my refrigerator. Check expiration dates on other yeast products you store.

COOKING WITH THE BASICS

Here are some foods you can make using just the basic items of food storage.

- ☐ Biscuits
- ☐ Bread
- ☐ Cookies
- ☐ Cooked cracked wheat
- ☐ Crackers
- ☐ Cream sauces
- ☐ Crepes
- ☐ Custards

- ☐ Muffins
- ☐ Pancakes
- ☐ Pasta
- ☐ Puddings
- ☐ Sprouted wheat
- ☐ Tortillas—whole-wheat, corn, and white flour varieties

STEP 3: FOODS FOR LONG-TERM STORAGE

You've made a list of foods and meals your family likes to eat. With that list in hand, let's review the different foods that do really well in storage. I have compiled items that have a long shelf life. You'll find canned, dehydrated, and freeze-dried options from all the food groups—fruits and vegetables, grains, proteins, and dairy—so that you'll be able to compose complete healthy meals. And I've included some special treats because we all need to delight our taste buds every now and then. I recommend that you try items that you've never eaten before. Maybe you love potatoes but dislike canned spuds. You don't want to stock up on foods you won't eat.

Keep in mind that when I give a shelf life, it's for an unopened can. Once you open that can, the shelf life of the food inside drops significantly. The shelf life of canned, freeze-dried, and dehydrated foods varies depending on the specific product and manufacturer. Check expiration dates, so you will be sure to use foods before they spoil.

Use this list below and the meal suggestions in "What to Cook" (page 56) to inform and inspire your personal food storage plan. Add items to your favorite foods list, make notes of things you want to taste, and meals you could make, and you will have come a long way in figuring out what foods to store.

VEGETABLES. Let's begin with vegetables since these are among the most nutritious foods you can eat. Just about every vegetable you'd want is available freeze-dried: broccoli, cauliflower, celery, red and green bell peppers, butternut squash, spinach, corn, zucchini, green beans, peas, asparagus, mushrooms, and onions. They are delicious and so easy to use. Most have a storage life of 25 years. I store some vegetables and fruits in dehydrated form, but I prefer freeze-dried because they don't need water to be edible. Dehydrated products need water and cooking to make them tasty. Also, in most cases, dehydrated foods have a shorter shelf life than freeze-dried foods—5 to 8 years compared to 20 to 25 years for freeze-dried foods. The only downside to freeze-dried foods is that they are more expensive.

Carrots. Carrots come dehydrated for storage and have an 8-year shelf life.

Potatoes. Canned, freeze-dried, or dehydrated—they are available in chunks, slices, or beads. Storage life for dehydrated or freeze-dried potatoes is approximately 20 years, though shorter for potato beads.

Sweet potatoes. Dehydrated sweet potatoes have an 8-year shelf life depending on the brand.

Tomatoes. You have so many options for storing tomatoes: canned, dehydrated, freeze-dried, paste, sauce, and flakes. Shelf life varies by product.

FRUITS. You can purchase freeze-dried raspberries, strawberries, pineapple, bananas, apples, oranges, cherries, grapes, cranberries, apricots, pears, blueberries, mangoes, and peaches. Be sure to stock up on fruit—it's nutritious and delicious. Most have a storage life of 25 years. Commercially dehydrated fruits generally have a shelf life of about 10 years if unopened and once opened they'll be good for about six months. Fruits and fruit leathers that are properly home dehydrated will last anywhere from six months to a year.

Applesauce. Most kids like applesauce and you can add it as a replacement for oil in equal amounts in muffin, cake, or cookie recipes without a noticeable difference in taste or texture. As with most canned products, the shelf life is usually under two years.

BEANS AND LEGUMES. They can be used in so many ways: soups, chili, enchiladas, rice and beans, salads, and as a side by themselves. Beans pack a lot of protein and fiber. I really like black, pinto, garbanzo, kidney, and white beans and lentils. They are available canned, instant, and dehydrated. I buy both canned beans from the supermarket when on sale, and #10 cans from food storage suppliers, but I store primarily instant beans in #10 cans because they use less water than regular dried beans—you don't have to soak them overnight and they cook in 20 minutes, thus using less water and fuel. My #10 cans of instant beans have a shelf life of 25 to 30 years. A #10 can of regular beans will last 10 or more years unopened, and the small cans you buy at the supermarket have an even shorter life. Bags of dried beans will last a year or more and are cheaper than canned, but of course, require water and take time to cook.

GRAINS AND GRAIN PRODUCTS. One of the five main food groups, whole grains are rich in nutrients and fiber and an important part of a healthy diet. Refined-grain products like white rice and white pasta are less nutritious but can still have a place at your plate.

Pasta. Spaghetti, elbows, bow ties—there are so many varieties, and if you purchase pasta commercially processed in #10 cans it will last for six to eight years. Macaroni and cheese is always popular. Make it from a box or from scratch. Add some green beans and fruit cocktail and you have a complete well-balanced meal. Whole-wheat pasta tends to go rancid quickly and should only be stored for about six months for the best flavor and for food safety.

Rice. Though brown rice, which retains its bran and germ layers, is more nutritious than white, it has a shorter shelf life—6 to 12 months. White rice can be stored for 4 to 5 years.

Quinoa. This is a truly remarkable food. It is one of the only plant foods that is a complete protein, providing all the essential amino acids. It is an excellent source of potassium, which has been associated with a healthy blood pressure, as well as magnesium, iron, vitamin B6, calcium, and fiber, and it's gluten-free. If you don't know this grain, you should get to know it. You'll find it in red, black, white, or yellow varieties, and most will last for 20 years. You might also consider Kamut and Teff—two other nutritious grains.

Chia. *(really a seed not a grain).* You may not find chia in most people's pantries, but I highly recommend it for its nutritional value. Chia is rich in heart-healthy omega-3 fatty acids and several minerals, including magnesium, plus it's high in fiber. You can add it to most recipes, including smoothies. Its shelf life is about two years.

Crackers. Bread has a short shelf life, so if you don't make your own, consider crackers, which last a little longer. You can top them with peanut butter and jelly or tuna. My grandkids love crackers with something spread on them. They feel like they are getting samples of food at the local grocery store. They love it, and so do I.

Ramen noodles. These cook up very fast. Add some meat and vegetables, and you have a main-meal soup in no time. Shelf life is usually about one year.

MEATS AND SEAFOOD. Tuna, chicken, roast beef, salmon, sardines, and other seafood come in cans. You also have the option of freeze-dried ham, sausage, chicken, turkey, roast beef, and ground beef. Reconstitute them and they taste terrific in casseroles, omelets, soups, and salads. The shelf life of meat and seafood depends on the product and manufacturer.

CHEESE AND OTHER DAIRY. Instant milk is a given; it's one of your staples, but did you know that you can also store freeze-dried cheese? It might not sound very appealing, but I use it all the time in my cooking and I love its convenience and flavor. You have several varieties to choose from: mozzarella, cheddar, Colby, Monterey Jack, and Parmesan. Shelf life is 10 to 25 years depending on the brand. Freeze-dried cheese must *always* be reconstituted in cold water. The texture of freeze-dried cheese is not exactly like regular dairy cheese but it works in casseroles. I have made grilled cheese sandwiches with reconstituted freeze-dried cheese and they were edible, but not the grilled cheese sandwiches we all know and love. To reconstitute freeze-dried cheese, I place it in cold water in a bowl for two to three minutes, drain it, place it in a plastic bag, and store it in the refrigerator until I'm ready to use it. It's definitely different from regular grated cheese.

Sour cream and cream cheese. These are also available freeze-dried and last 5 to 10 years in storage. I recommend you only make a small batch of the sour cream or cream cheese as needed, because without preservatives it will not stay fresh as long as regular sour cream or cream cheese. Both are great for use in cooking and dips.

Yogurt. You can purchase freeze-dried yogurt bites, which will keep for 3 to 5 years in storage. Eat them right out of the package or reconstitute them with water for texture closer to the original.

CANNED MEALS. Canned chili, ravioli, spaghetti, and other meals are edible right out of the can if you don't have a means of heating them. Storage life is usually shorter on canned products like these so check expiration dates.

FREEZE-DRIED MEALS. A few companies make freeze-dried meals. Some of these meals include dehydrated vegetables or TVP (textured vegetable protein). Check the ingredients list to see if the product is what you're expecting it to be. If you can't pronounce the ingredients, think before you buy.

SOUPS. Cream of chicken and cream of mushroom are staples in my house. You can eat them on their own or add them to casseroles. There are so many varieties of canned soups and those made with meat, vegetables and pasta or rice are meals in themselves. Canned soups have a short shelf life so check expiration dates.

SPREADS AND CONDIMENTS. Because sometimes foods need a little flavor boost.

Mayonnaise, mustard, and ketchup. These have a shelf life that is usually under two years. Once mayonnaise is opened, it must be refrigerated so if you lose electricity you'll be eating tuna without mayo. I buy mayo in small containers in case of a power outage so I will waste as little as possible. You can purchase cases of single-serve packets of mayonnaise, Miracle Whip, pickle relish, mustard, and ketchup, which would be better than bottles for storage. I would recommend storing them no longer than six to eight months. Another option is to make ketchup with powdered tomato or tomato flakes. Mustard can be whipped up using mustard powder, vinegar, and spices. Check your condiments to see if they require refrigeration after opening. If they do and the power goes out, don't use them.

Jam and jellies. I prefer to buy smaller jars, because if we lose power I would rather not have a 32-ounce (960-g) jar of jam sitting on the counter without refrigeration. Most jams and jellies can be stored for one to two years.

Peanut butter. I usually have 12 jars in my storage room at all times. It's a great source of protein and healthy fats. I don't buy large jars anymore since the kids have grown up and moved out. Peanut butter can go rancid, so check expiration dates and don't store more jars than your family can eat in a year. You can also purchase peanut butter in powder form. A #10 can has a shelf life of 5 to 10 years.

Pickles. I love pickles—on a sandwich, in macaroni salad, in relish. And I eat both dill and sweet, but their shelf life is short—just one to two years.

Gravy. I never thought I would buy gravy in jars but I do. It tastes awesome and it cuts down dinner preparation considerably. You can purchase chicken, turkey, and beef gravy. Check the expiration date on the jar or can.

SNACKS AND SPECIAL TREATS. I don't want you to think of food storage only in terms of survival. Plan for pleasure, too. Purchase items you enjoy eating for snacks or the occasional dessert.

Cocoa for baking and for hot cocoa. I like to store my cocoa in a 1-gallon (3.78-L) container, and it will keep for about a year after it's been opened. Cocoa has a shelf life of about two years if unopened, though it depends on the brand and the storage temperature. It might be safe to consume beyond that, but the quality and flavor may not be very good.

Cookie, cake, and other mixes: Mixes are a great short-term food storage item to have on hand if you have a means to bake them (see Chapter 3 for information on emergency cooking appliances). Just add water and bake.

Granola bars: There are so many types of granola bars, protein bars, and other snack bars that are great to have on hand if you need a quick grab-and-go breakfast or snack.

Nuts. They pack a lot of protein and calories, so a small serving goes a long way in keeping you feeling full and satisfied. They're also rich in monounsaturated fats, which promote good cholesterol. Shelf life isn't terrific—only about 12 months in an unopened container—so be sure to rotate them for maximum storage time.

Popcorn. It's a yummy snack that's also healthful (if you don't drench it in butter), providing lots of fiber, and it will last indefinitely. Skip microwave popcorn—It only lasts 6 to 8 months and isn't as wholesome as regular popped popcorn.

WHIPPING CREAM IN A BOX. This is a special treat for your family. It comes in liquid form in a carton that you can store for up to six months (watch that expiration date!) on your shelves. Before using, chill it for about eight hours and then pour the contents of the carton into a bowl, add vanilla, and whip. The whipped cream must be stored in the refrigerator and used within 24 hours.

WHAT TO COOK

Here are several ideas for meals and sides you can make using the items I've recommended in my foods-to-store list.

- ☐ Bean burritos
- ☐ Bean salads
- ☐ Bean soup, with or without meat
- ☐ Bread
- ☐ Casseroles made with chicken or turkey, broccoli, and rice
- ☐ Cheesy potatoes
- ☐ Chicken with vegetables
- ☐ Chicken salad, or substitute tuna, salmon, or ham
- ☐ Chili, red or white chicken chili, homemade
- ☐ Cinnamon rolls
- ☐ Cookies, cakes, muffins, and pies
- ☐ Enchiladas
- ☐ Fruit sauces
- ☐ Granola with fruit
- ☐ Ham and bean soup, homemade
- ☐ Hamburger, vegetable, and tomato soup, homemade
- ☐ Macaroni and cheese
- ☐ Macaroni salads
- ☐ Monkey bread with butter, brown sugar, and cinnamon

- ☐ Monkey bread with herbs, garlic, Parmesan cheese, and butter
- ☐ Peanut butter and jelly sandwiches
- ☐ Peanut butter and honey sandwiches
- ☐ Pizza
- ☐ Popcorn or caramel corn
- ☐ Salads
- ☐ Salsa
- ☐ Sausage and gravy over biscuits
- ☐ Shepherd's pie
- ☐ Sloppy Joes with homemade buns
- ☐ Spaghetti with or without meat sauce
- ☐ Tacos with homemade tortillas and freeze-dried beef
- ☐ Tamale Pie
- ☐ Taquitos made with homemade tortillas, beans, meat, and cheese
- ☐ Tortillas and tortilla chips
- ☐ Tuna casserole
- ☐ Quiche
- ☐ Quinoa salads or sides
- ☐ Waffles

STEP 4: WRITE A WEEK'S WORTH OF MEAL PLANS

Once you have a good list going of what everyone likes to eat (and keep adding to this list as you discover new foods), I suggest developing some meal plans to help guide your food storage efforts. Your family may love tuna fish, canned peaches, pasta, and canned green beans but you won't want to eat them for breakfast, lunch, and dinner. Let's just take seven days of meal planning to make this fairly easy. Work from Sunday through Saturday writing down what meal you'll have for breakfast, lunch, and dinner. If family members like to grab a snack between meals, include those as well. Every family has different needs, and you'll want to consider not only what everyone likes to eat but what they should eat based on overall good nutrition, calorie needs, health issues, and food allergies.

Writing up a week's meal plan makes it easier to figure out what foods to store, but it's also just a good practice to get in the habit of doing regularly. It makes grocery shopping more efficient, and it can be a real money saver if done right. I plan at least a week ahead not only to make sure I have the foods I need for the meals I want to prepare but also to incorporate and replace stored foods. You don't want to simply pack away your canned and freeze-dried goods and forget about them until an emergency occurs. You want to use them and replace them to prevent spoilage as well as become accustomed to eating them and cooking with them. Here's how I think through my meal plans and food storage.

BREAKFAST

My husband and I eat cereal, oatmeal, pancakes, waffles, eggs, bacon, smoothies, and muffins regularly, so I stock up on the following:

EGGS AND BACON: I keep eggs and bacon in the refrigerator for day-to-day use, but I also have powdered eggs for storage and use it when I run out of fresh eggs. I do have commercially canned bacon, but I will only use that as a treat because it is so expensive.

CEREAL: I typically buy three months' worth of cereal at a time.

FRUITS AND VEGETABLES FOR SMOOTHIES: I store freeze-dried produce, and when the growing season is over, I'll pull from my stash, making sure to replace what I use.

MILK FOR CEREAL AND SMOOTHIES: I use store-bought milk from day to day, but I also use #10 cans of instant milk. Add water, and it's ready to use when I run out of the milk that's in my fridge.

PANCAKES AND WAFFLES: I can make them from scratch, but I want a mix as well that I can simply add water to and cook on the griddle. I like jam or maple syrup on top, so I store small containers of both.

MUFFINS: Mixes are a great short-term food storage item to have on hand if you have a means to bake them (see Chapter 3 for information on emergency cooking appliances). Just add water and bake.

GRANOLA BARS: These are handy if we need something quick to grab on the run.

LUNCH

I make my own bread, so my husband and I typically have sandwiches for lunch.

BREAD: To make bread in an emergency situation, I store the hard white whole wheat that I use.

MEAT: I buy very little deli meat because it spoils quickly. Instead I stock up on canned tuna, chicken, and roast beef that I mix with a little mayonnaise or mustard.

PEANUT BUTTER AND JELLY: A kid favorite, peanut butter and jelly (or jam) sandwiches are fantastic for adults, too.

SIDES: I store both canned and freeze-dried vegetables and fruits, both of which can be eaten straight out of the container. My husband and I love pickles, and keep several jars around.

DINNER

Usually we have some sort of protein, salad, and fruit for dinner. We also often eat pasta or beans with our meal. I stock up on plenty of foods that don't require refrigeration in case we lose electricity.

MEAT: I grew up on Spam and canned salmon. I've never bought those since I've been married, for some reason, but my neighbors love them. I only buy canned tuna, chicken, and roast beef, and since I use these for sandwiches, as well, I need to make sure I have storage for both meals.

BEANS: I like white beans, black beans, kidney beans, and pinto beans to eat on their own or to add to soups or stews, and I store #10 cans of instant beans, which need just a little water added and cook up quickly.

VEGETABLES: I buy canned potatoes, green beans, corn, diced tomatoes, and Rotel tomatoes. I also like to use some of my freeze-dried or dehydrated vegetables (potatoes, green beans, corn, tomatoes, cauliflower, broccoli, asparagus, sweet potatoes, celery, bell peppers, and onions) so that I know how to use them on a daily basis instead of waiting for an emergency to figure out which ones taste good.

FRUITS: My favorite canned fruits include peaches, mandarin oranges, pineapple, pears, and fruit cocktail. I make sure to include lots of freeze-dried fruits in my meals, too—bananas, apples, pineapple, peaches, pears, strawberries, raspberries, grapes, or blackberries. My family loves to eat freeze-dried pineapple straight from the #10 cans.

PASTA, RICE, AND OTHER GRAINS: We eat almost any type of pasta as well as rice, cooked wheat, and quinoa with our meals. If the power goes out, I can boil water on my butane stove (only butane stoves can be used indoors).

SOUPS: I always have on hand cream of chicken soup, cream of mushroom soup, and tomato soup, which my husband and I can heat and eat or combine with other ingredients for a complete meal.

MEALS IN A CAN: I don't want to eat this stuff every day, but in an emergency I would love a can of ravioli, spaghetti, beef stew, or chili, so I include them in my food storage.

CONDIMENTS: I buy enchilada sauce, salsa, mayonnaise, Miracle Whip, barbecue sauce, tartar sauce, mustard, and ketchup.

TREATS

I'm crazy for chocolate and I store leftover Halloween candy in a jar with a tight lid.

On page 35 is a sample of a sheet that I've developed to make it easy to create a week's worth of menus and a list of the foods you'll need for each meal. You can go to my blog, foodstoragemoms.com, and download several of these sheets free. Involve your whole family in meal planning and food storage, so that everyone's wants and needs are captured in your plan. Besides, it's more fun when you do it together.

GOOD NUTRITION FOR GOOD HEALTH

When planning meals and what foods to store, follow the same sound nutrition guidelines that you use, hopefully, in your day-to-day eating.

☐ Include lots of vegetables and fruits and a wide variety of them. They are nutrition powerhouses, packed with vitamins, minerals, and other nutrients such as disease-fighting antioxidants. In addition, they are an excellent source of fiber, which is important for a healthy digestive system.

☐ Choose whole grains. They are also an important source of nutrients including several B vitamins, the minerals iron, magnesium, and selenium, and fiber.

☐ Pick lean proteins primarily, which are low in heart-unhealthy saturated fats. Poultry, pork, fish, beans, and other legumes are your best options.

☐ Opt for olive oil, canola oil, or other monounsaturated fats, which help raise levels of good cholesterol and have been shown to be a part of a heart-healthy diet.

YOUR STORAGE SPACE

One of the questions you'll need to ask early on in your food storage preparation is where are you going to store all this stuff?

If you have a food pantry in your home, begin there. The shelves in my pantry were placed too far apart for efficient storage. There was a lot of wasted space, so I evaluated the size of the items I was storing, had new shelves made, and arranged them so that when I stocked the shelves there would be little leftover space. I packed my pantry to the max. Take a look at your own pantry and see if you can rearrange it to better use the space for storage.

BASEMENTS AND OTHER PLACES

Basements are one of the best places to store food. They tend to be cooler and darker than the rest of the house, which is ideal since the shelf life of most foods is extended in those conditions. Also, the temperature of basement space stays more consistent than the rest of the house without a lot of highs and lows as seasons change. Look for water leakage around windows and floors and patch any that you find; water will rust metal cans and damage cardboard boxes. And check for critters—insects, mice, whatever creature might be interested in making a meal of your grains, fruits, and vegetables. Food in cans and plastic containers should be safe, but anything stored in bags of any kind is at risk of being

We all wish we had more space to store our stuff. Consider using that front closet or empty bedroom as space to store your emergency food. Be creative.

gnawed through. If you choose to store your foods in the basement, lay down pallets or some other platform on the floor beneath them to prevent rust from developing on the bottoms of cans and mold from growing on boxed goods.

My husband and I don't store any foodstuffs in our garage or shed, because it gets so hot here in southern Utah much of the year. Although well insulated, our garage will heat up to over 90°F (32°C) during the day from early June through August each year. We do use the extra space in our garage (we park just one car) to store all our other emergency preparation items, though. The temperatures in an attic can get extremely hot as well. I do not recommend storing food in your attic unless it is insulated and has air-conditioning to keep it at a cool and safe temperature for storage.

GETTING CREATIVE IN SMALL SPACES

Those of us with limited living and storage space will need to be very creative when it comes to storing for emergency preparedness. Friends of ours faced such challenging space issues that they made bookshelves out of cans of food and would stack cases of soup, and covered them with tablecloths for end tables and coffee tables. They even set the box springs and mattresses of their beds on top of cases of canned goods.

My husband and I stretched the finances a bit and bought some nice movable shelving that holds 56 #10 cans and has good-quality casters on its base. We have strategically placed four of these units in our bunk-bed room for easy access. When our grandkids come to stay, we wheel two units into our bedroom so the kids can use the bunk beds. It's not ideal but our home is small so we have to make the most of the space we have. We also place filled WaterBricks under our queen-size bed and have 56 gallons (212.8-L) of water stored there. If you live in an apartment or small home, put on your thinking cap as you walk from room to room devising creative ways to store food and water.

SHELVING

Good shelving makes all the difference in the world when it comes to easy and efficient food storage. In one of our former homes we built our own shelving along a basement wall. We used good-quality 2 x 4's (0.6-1.2 M) for the sides and supports and then particleboard for the shelves. We designed these units so the shelves would tilt slightly forward, added a small molding along the front to prevent the cans from rolling off onto the floor. This design allows you to store cans on their sides, and as you remove the can in front, the others will roll forward. As you replenish, you'll put the freshest cans at the back of the row, so that you are always using your oldest food first. Another advantage to the tilted shelf is that as your cans roll forward, the food inside gets tumbled, making it less likely to solidify.

You don't have to make your own shelves. You can buy metal units with or without tilted shelves, depending on your preference. Shelving that's designed specifically for food storage usually has slots of varying widths to fit cans of different sizes. You'll want to be sure the unit you buy will work with the size cans you purchase. When you build these, be sure all the bolts and connections are secure to prevent accidents. One of the advantages of metal shelving is that you can take it apart and take it with you if you move.

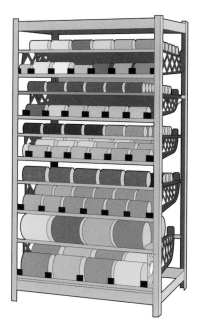

Shelving comes in many shapes and sizes. When purchasing your storage shelves, be sure to consider what size cans need to be stored, how you plan to rotate, and how important being able to move them is to your family.

FOOD ROTATION

There's an old adage that goes, "Eat what you store and store what you eat." Follow this rule and you'll never waste any of the food you buy. Remember, food storage isn't about just stocking up for an emergency and then letting all that food sit unused until you need it. Using it in your daily life and rotating it is an important part of emergency preparation. Some products have incredibly long shelf lives, but the easiest way to make sure everything stays edible is to eat a little of what you've stored on a regular basis. If you set a goal to use some of these foods at least twice a week, you'll not only follow a reasonable rotation schedule, but you'll be very familiar with what you have in storage, what needs to be replaced, and which foods you eat most often and therefore they may need a larger inventory.

Using shelves that slant forward makes rotating foods simple because you'll pull the oldest can from the front and replenish by putting the newest can at the back. I store all my foods in alphabetical order to make it easier to find what I need, and it helps me quickly review what I have on hand so that I can purchase foods in the right quantities. I've also made some checklists to help me keep track of what I've used and what I need to buy.

I've covered a lot of information in this chapter and I hope that if at first you felt daunted by food storage, you now see that it is very doable and simple if you approach it with a well-thought-out list of foods to store, purchase them gradually as your budget allows, and store them properly. I hope that you'll begin today or tomorrow or even the next day with this well-laid path for food storage in front of you.

PAPER, PLASTIC, OR PORCELAIN?

I store paper plates, hot cups, cold cups, straws, napkins, and plastic utensils, and I have thousands. But I also have 32 somewhat nonbreakable dishes along with stainless steel flatware. What I use will depend on the water issues at hand.

FOOD FOR FIDO

Your dog or cat is a member of your family, right? So don't forget that you'll need to store pet food, too. Keep track of how much your pet eats in a week and then begin creating a stash of food to feed him or her in an emergency. If you have farm animals or exotic pets, don't forget to store food for them, too. As with your own food storage plan, build gradually as your budget allows. The next time you go to the grocery store, buy an extra can or bag of pet food and put it aside, then add to it over time.

BUDGETING FOR FOOD STORAGE

Every family should have a budget to help them make the most of their income, and if food storage is important to you, I suggest that you make it one of the line items in your accounting. I understand that some families have limited resources and may even live paycheck to paycheck. When you look at your income and expenses, you may not see how you could possibly make room in your budget for buying foods to store. If emergency preparedness is a priority, put your spending under the microscope. Are there ways you can trim your expenses?

Maybe cut back on entertainment. Watch movies at home instead of in the theater. Search for free local concerts instead of paid events. Create a vacation at home this year instead of planning a trip. Stretch out the time between hair appointments. Buy tops, skirts, pants, sweaters, and jackets that you can mix and match so you can look fresh with fewer clothes.

The cost of phones has skyrocketed today with every family member wanting or needing a cell phone. I know people who have canceled their landlines and only use their cell phones. And speaking of those cell phones, we are bombarded constantly with enticing ads for the latest and greatest technology, but you don't have to have the best. Consider purchasing less expensive models (it is possible to get a decent smartphone that is not an Android or Apple) and shopping for a reasonably priced phone plan.

Think about how you might trim your food and dining expenses. This is one of the biggest line items in most families' budgets. Does your family drink soda? Cut back or, better yet, cut it out altogether. Just drive past the coffee shop rather than head to the drive-through to buy your favorite latte. Cook meals at home and reserve dining out and takeout for special occasions. And watch your newspapers or search online for coupons. Whatever money you are able to save on your current food spending, you can put toward food storage.

If these measures seem insignificant to you as you think about saving and spending for emergency preparedness, remember my motto: buy one can at a time.

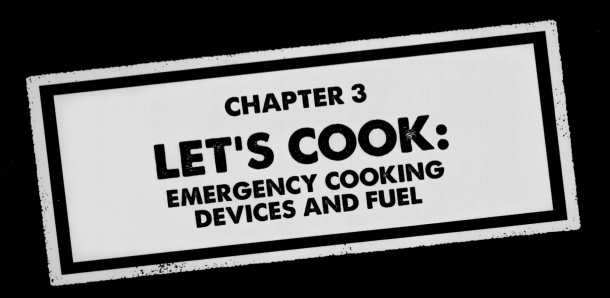

CHAPTER 3
LET'S COOK:
EMERGENCY COOKING DEVICES AND FUEL

When the power grid goes down, the burners on your stove go cold. If you're not prepared with some alternatives to your indoor range and oven, get ready to relive your campfire days or settle for meals out of a can.

In this chapter, you'll learn what kinds of cooking devices are best for emergencies, what types of fuel you'll need, and even how to make your own fire starters. You'll be ready to continue serving your family hot meals no matter the situation.

We are so fortunate to be able to go into our kitchens and turn the dial on our electric or gas stove and start cooking or even just heat up water for tea. And let's not forget the fabulous microwave—if you have leftover beef stew from last night's dinner, it will be ready to eat in minutes. But what will you do if the power goes out? If you have a gas stove, you may be able to light it with a match, though that's not the safest thing to do, but if your oven and range work off electricity, you could be without a way to cook food or boil water for days, weeks, possibly longer. Yes, you can eat tuna and ravioli out of a can and freeze-dried fruits and vegetables right from the container, but it won't be long before that gets old. And hopefully you've stored lots of water, but what if you run out and need to boil water to purify it for drinking? To be well prepared for emergency situations, it's wise to have a backup cooking device as well as the proper fuel to use with it.

COOKING APPLIANCES

If you read the food storage chapter and were wondering how you were going to make those hot meals and baked goods I suggested you include in your food plan, well, here's how—invest in one of these cooking appliances. You may be surprised at the variety of options available, including outdoor ovens. And you are probably familiar enough with me at this point in the book to know that having an oven is a must so that I can keep baking homemade bread no matter what the situation. I keep several different emergency cooking appliances because each has its own specialty, and having a few devices, each using different types of fuel, gives me more options in an emergency and allows me to stretch my fuel stores to the max. Think about what kind of cooking and baking you do most often and explore the options here to find the appliance with the features that best meet your needs, but I recommend everyone start by purchasing a butane stove. It's inexpensive, and it's the only option for indoor cooking.

COUNTERTOP BUTANE STOVE

For indoor cooking, you'll want a countertop-style butane stove. They are simple to use. You remove the red cap on the fuel canister, insert it into the stove, and lock it in place. With a turn of the dial, you have a flame, and you're ready to cook. Call me a nervous Nellie but even though butane is a safe fuel to use indoors, I like to open my windows a crack. These stoves are portable, so you can use them on your patio or take them on a camping trip, and they're inexpensive, typically running less than $30. How long the butane canister will last depends on how much you use the stove. With periodic use, one canister lasts me a few weeks. I buy them in 12 packs so I have plenty around.

Use: indoors or outdoors

Fuel: butane

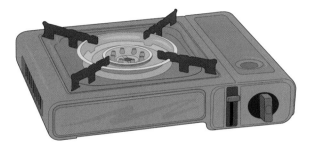

Small butane stoves you can use on your countertop provide a whole new option for emergency cooking indoors and outside.

GAS BARBECUE OR GRILL

My first choice for cooking outdoors in an emergency situation would be the gas barbecue, which you may already have; most families do. In addition to grilling, you can place your cast-iron pots, griddles, and Dutch ovens right on the grate to heat up water or soup or scramble some eggs. Make sure you have pans that can be used on a grill because you wouldn't want to ruin your fancy cookware if it isn't safe for open-fire cooking. I do not recommend water bath or pressure canning on a gas grill, because you can't control the constant temperature needed for canning food safely. Most barbecues have a temperature gauge built into the lid, but remember it is not always accurate; simply follow your recipe for temperature settings and cooking time.

I try to keep a minimum of one extra propane tank ready to exchange when needed and I only buy the small ones that go with our barbecue. Propane tanks are heavy when filled with fuel. The large ones that you see on RVs seem like they'd be great, but you need to be able to haul them to wherever your barbecue is located, which may require a dolly.

Use: outdoors only

Fuel: propane

CHARCOAL BARBECUE

A small charcoal grill works well for individuals or families who have only a balcony or small patio available for cooking outdoors, and they can be used in the same ways as a larger barbecue. Charcoal tabletop barbecues are inexpensive, so they are a good option if you are concerned about price. The cheaper units do not have any adjustment for heat and may not tell the temperature. Larger units—though more costly—have much more surface area for cooking, and are likely to have options to tell temperature and adjust heat. It's important to remember to *never* use charcoal grills indoors because the fumes would be toxic in an enclosed environment.

Use: outdoors only

Fuel: charcoal briquettes, lump charcoal, or wood

That barbecue you've relied on for weekend parties can also be a lifesaver when other options for cooking aren't available.

THERMAL COOKER

This device works much like a slow cooker but without electricity. It has an inner stainless steel pot that fits inside the thermal cooker. You place the foods you are going to cook—meat and vegetables, chili ingredients, soup ingredients, whatever—inside the stainless steel pan, cover them with water, bring everything to a boil on top of your stove, and boil for 4 minutes—and I'm talking about a full rolling boil. Then you put the pot of food inside the thermal cooker and tighten the lid. Food will continue to cook without any additional heat source.

I highly recommend that you have a butane stove to use with the thermal cooker. In case of a power outage, this is a great combination because you can use the butane stove to boil water, make soup, or heat up a can of chili very quickly. Then you can use the thermal cooker to finish cooking the food with zero additional energy.

As I've mentioned with other emergency-preparedness items, it's a good idea to get comfortable using the thermal cooker *before* an emergency. These cookers are portable, so you can take only a few minutes to start a hot meal at home and let it cook while you are away from home. Some ideas are using it for a picnic, on a long road trip, or camping. Parents could be cooking dinner in their cars while they're watching their kids' sports games. You might not have a lot of time for food preparation, but hopefully you do have time to gather some of your foodstuffs and heat water, then you use the thermal cooker to actually cook the food, whether you stay in one place or not. Using a thermal cooker is an excellent way to be prepared for emergencies while also saving energy.

Use: indoors or outdoors

Fuel: uses the heat from the ingredients in the pot to cook food, so it must be accompanied by a stove, such as a butane stove, to bring the water and other ingredients to a boil.

Thermal cookers are a must-have for today's busy families. They are a good resource when the "what am I going to do now?" meal preparation issue comes up.

KELLY KETTLE

One of my favorite stoves is the Kelly Kettle. The only fuel you'll need are twigs, newspaper, pinecones, or other kindling, and it's easy to keep adding them to feed the flame. I can boil water in about 3 minutes using very little fuel. It has two pieces: a firebase and a kettle. You simply pour water in the kettle, put your flammable material in the base, light it, and then place the kettle on top. In just minutes you'll have boiling water for hot cocoa or soup, and you can purchase a Hobo Stove and a cooking kit to prepare meals. Popular for camping, the Kelly Kettle is made from sturdy aluminum or stainless steel, is lightweight, and packs easily for transport or storage.

Portable stoves like the Kelly Kettle work efficiently and quickly with very little fuel.

Use: outdoors only

Fuel: pinecones, twigs, newspaper, any type of kindling

CAMPCHEF STOVES

CampChef is widely known and loved. This manufacturer makes stoves with one, two, three, or four burners that are sturdy enough to hold Dutch ovens and even my heavy-duty pressure canner in case we've had a power outage and I need to preserve food from my garden. One of the features I love is the optional griddle top. I can cook whole-wheat pancakes for the whole neighborhood, and, yes, I have lots of maple syrup. Another useful feature of these stoves is that they are portable and fold up neatly into a case so you can take them with you when you go camping.

Use: outdoors only

Fuel: propane

CampChef stoves provide great flexibility for cooking food on weekends or in emergency situations.

A TRIAL RUN

If you've purchased a cooking device that you've never used before, don't wait for an emergency to learn how it works. Try it out at least once or several times to become comfortable using it. Many of these devices are portable—maybe you'll be inspired to take that camping trip that you keep putting off because you've been unsure how to best handle cooking in the woods. Pack your new stove and enjoy.

Having a versatile stove/oven combo gives you a wider range of foods you can prepare in a disaster.

CAMPCHEF COMBINATION STOVE AND OVEN

If you need an oven like I do to bake bread, you should consider the Deluxe Outdoor Oven by CampChef. While you're baking, you can use the burners on top to boil water, heat soup, or make a stovetop meal. This unit can be used with small propane canisters or the tanks typically used with a grill. Make sure you have the correct adapter for the canister or tank that you decide to use. This oven is also portable for use on camping trips.

Use: outdoors only

Fuel: propane

VOLCANO GRILL

For fuel versatility, you might consider the Volcano 3. It's a collapsible grill roughly 11 inches (28 cm) high and 13 inches (33 cm) in diameter at the top, and it collapses to 5 inches (12 cm) for storage. You can use propane, wood, or charcoal briquettes with it. I love having a cooking device that allows me more than one option for fuel. You can purchase a tentlike cover that traps and circulates heat for baking. I don't use it for bread though because I don't want that grill flavor in my bread. If you decide to purchase a Volcano, check out the adapters. Some stoves come with only one adapter, and you will want to make sure your adapter works with the propane tank or canisters you purchase.

Use: outdoors only

Fuel: propane, wood, or charcoal briquettes

Volcano stoves use wood, charcoal, or propane for fuel, and they can be used for baking.

SOLAR OVEN

Now let's talk solar cooking. I have two All American Sun Ovens because, living in southern Utah as I do, I can cook many meals without using any fuel, and I can bake four loaves of bread at a time—two loaves in each oven. Keep in mind that the best time to cook in one of these is between 10:00 a.m. and 3:00 p.m. when the sun is the hottest. The time zones and seasons will influence your optimal cooking hours. If you get very little sunshine where you live, I wouldn't purchase one of these.

If you have sunshine, you can bake the same food as your conventional oven during an emergency.

You can make any meal in a solar oven that you would bake in a conventional oven and you can reheat food, but you can't sauté or fry foods. I like to cook pasta in mine because I can simply bring the water to a boil, toss in the pasta, and let it cook. Forty-five minutes later, the pasta is cooked to perfection.

Use: outdoors only

Fuel: sunlight (how cool is that!)

OPEN-FIRE COOKING

Some families have fire pits on their patios or in their yards to add a special touch to their landscaping and a gathering place to cook hot dogs and roast marshmallows. If you can find a spot where a small fire pit can be located safely, it just adds to your options for cooking in an emergency situation. They can be made with bricks, stone, or a metal frame to contain the wood or briquettes used for cooking, or your fire pit can be as simple as a hole in the ground. Set some wood or charcoal in the pit, light it, and you're ready for an outdoor adventure in cooking.

I highly recommend that you use a Dutch oven (details on these a little later in this chapter) when cooking over an open flame. They heat foods more evenly and are easier to clean than the standard kitchen pots and pans that are thinner and become so blackened from cooking that it becomes very difficult to clean them without scratching the surface. In an emergency, if all that you have is your regular cookware, then go ahead and use it, but since our goal with this book is to prepare in advance, consider adding a Dutch oven to your emergency-preparedness list.

When you're cooking over a fire, let the flame die down and place your Dutch oven filled with whatever food you're preparing right on the coals. You might consider buying or making a cooking stand so you can hang the Dutch oven above the coals. The stand needs to be sturdy so it can handle the weight of the pot and all of its contents.

Another option for open-fire cooking is to prepare what many call hobo dinners. Cut up vegetables and meats, add some seasoning, wrap them all up in aluminum foil, and place them right on the coals in your fire pit or grill. It can be a challenge figuring out how long to cook these meals, but other than that it's simple and it works.

Use: outdoors only

Fuel: wood or charcoal

FUEL FOR THE FIRE

The best cooking device money can buy won't be any use without fuel. And it's important to know how to store it and use it safely. Let's take a closer look at the different fuels you might use with your grills, stoves, and ovens.

PROPANE

Propane lasts indefinitely, so I highly recommend having a propane-based grill or stove in case of a long-term emergency situation. Always check your tanks for any rust or dents and when you go to have them filled ask the personnel to check the valves and make sure they are in good working order. I prefer to have my propane containers filled by authorized companies rather than buy the more expensive prefilled tanks. Store them upright, preferably on a concrete slab, and outside, not in your garage—propane is extremely flammable.

BUTANE

Terrific for boiling water and heating foods that require short cooking times, butane is the only fuel you can use safely indoors (although I still crack a window when using my butane stove). Check the tip of the canister; if it's broken or damaged, you won't be able to use it. Butane comes in small canisters, and it's hard to say how long they will last, so I buy these in packages of 12 and I store them in my shed.

CHARCOAL

You can purchase lump charcoal or briquettes. Lump charcoal is made from tree branches, twigs, and scraps of hardwood from lumber mills that are cooked or charred in low-oxygen conditions in kilns or silos. Charcoal briquettes are made from sawdust and wood chips that are also cooked and charred and then mixed with bits of coal and other natural additives so the material can be molded into briquettes. Lump charcoal burns more slowly, stays hotter longer, and produces less ash than briquettes. Both will last indefinitely if kept dry. I buy oak lump charcoal as well as briquettes without the starter chemicals embedded in them. While both are good for cooking, the lump charcoal would stay hotter longer if we need it to keep us warm, and the briquettes are best for Dutch-oven cooking. I store both types of charcoal in five-gallon plastic buckets with Gamma Seal Lids. These lids are made of heavy-duty plastic and create an airtight seal on most 12-inch (30 cm) diameter 5-gallon (19-L) plastic pails, and they're reusable.

PINECONES

As I mentioned earlier, pinecones can be used as fuel in the Kelly Kettle, and the only cost is your time and effort to collect them. Once you've gathered them, it's best to bake them to clean off the sap and kill any insects that might be hiding inside. First I hose off the pinecones outside and let them dry; then I place them on a cookie sheet covered with aluminum foil and bake them at 200°F (93°C) for two hours. I cool them overnight and store them in black plastic buckets with black Gamma Seal Lids.

STORE THIS ADVICE

- ☐ Your city or county government has requirements for how and where fuel can be stored on your property. Find out what they are and then follow them.
- ☐ Color-coding makes identification easier. I have several 5-gallon (19-L) buckets with Gamma Seal Lids in different colors that I use for storing supplies. For example, I use red with lump charcoal, blue with briquettes, and black for pinecones.

WOOD

If there's a place nearby where you can cut and gather wood yourself, that's awesome, but you'll need a chain saw and a truck to haul the logs to your home where you'll need to split them into usable pieces. Otherwise you can buy wood and have it delivered. Sometimes you can pick up free raw wood scraps from cabinet-making companies, but don't take wood that has been painted or stained; it will release chemicals in your home or around your food as you burn it.

FIRE STARTERS

A turn of the knob will ignite a flame in most propane and butane-fueled cooking appliances, but starting a fire in a charcoal grill or fire pit is done manually, and you can get a helping hand from a fire starter. There are several options, and all of them will help you get your fire started faster and hotter than if you simply light a match to the wood or the briquette. Of course, you do still need matches.

HOMEMADE

I like making fire starters from used materials I have in my home because they're inexpensive, and it makes good use of something that might otherwise end up in the trash. Here's one of my favorites: I save empty toilet paper rolls and fill them with cotton balls, then roll them in waxed paper and twist the ends to keep the cotton balls inside. (I've also tried this with dryer lint in place of the cotton balls, but the flame went out too quickly.) You can make the same type of starter with plastic straws, although it's a bit more laborious. Cut them into 3-to-4-inch (8-10 cm) lengths and stuff them with pieces of cotton balls coated with petroleum jelly. Store them in airtight containers.

I also make what I call newspaper twists for starting fires. Take a few sheets of newspaper and roll them tightly, fold the rolled paper in half and tie it with natural jute twine. When my family would hike up into the mountains, we'd take these along to start a fire for roasting marshmallows. I store newspaper twists in airtight containers to keep them dry.

COMMERCIAL

There are several types of commercial fire starters. One uses a flintlike substance with a striking device. Strike the flint on the device next to dry twigs, paper, or other flammable material, and the spark will start a small fire. Another product I like is Instafire. It's made with recycled wood, volcanic rock, and safe-to-use paraffin wax. Simply light it with a match, and it's ready to use. I have been able to use this product in the snow without a stove or any bricks to protect the flame, and it will burn for almost an hour. Yes, you read that correctly, it burns in cold, icy snow. It's great for camping as well as emergency situations. Instafire comes in small packages or loose in 5-gallon (19-L) containers and lasts indefinitely if stored in a dry environment. I find the packages more convenient, and I store them in 5-gallon (19-L) buckets with Gamma Seal Lids.

Another option to consider—fire starter fuel disks. I like the Cloudy Day Fuel Disks/Fire Starters available at Sunoven.com. They are made from recycled materials, are nontoxic, and completely waterproof—you can even light them in the rain. They catch fire in seconds, will reach a temperature of 1,200°F (649°C) within two minutes, and burn for approximately 45 minutes in wind, rain, or snow. You can use them to start a charcoal or wood fire, as an emergency heat source outside, and you can boil water in a pan placed right on top of the disk. They store indefinitely.

POTS AND PANS

Your kitchen cookware will work just fine on a butane stove, but it might not be made to withstand the rigors of outdoor cooking on the barbecue or charcoal grill, and an open fire pit presents a real challenge. Plastic handles may not survive the high temperatures, and the pots themselves may become so blackened over a fire that you'll never see that shiny surface again. Cooking outdoors can be a little or a lot rugged and you'll want to use some rough and tough cookware with heat-resistant handles and thicker material that can take a beating. I use cast-iron pots, griddles, fry pans, and Dutch ovens because they meet the requirements needed to cook over open flames or with briquettes and are solidly made. Some cookware other than cast iron can work just fine over open flames; check the manufacturer's instructions.

Be sure to wear well-insulated mitts to protect your hands when lifting or moving a pan of food from Point A to Point B. You can also use silicone handle holders that make it so easy to pick up cast iron, which can get very hot. When working with cast-iron Dutch ovens that have a thin rotating handle, it's best to use a special metal Dutch-oven lifter, which is designed to lift these pots or the lids. Using the lifter also allows extra distance from your hands to the flame or heat source so you're less likely to get burned.

CAST-IRON COOKWARE AND DUTCH OVENS

I love cooking with a Dutch oven, and I am sure you will, too, if you don't already. The Dutch oven is a large, heavy cooking pot with a lid. It's usually made of cast iron so it's thick, cooks food evenly, and can withstand very high temperatures. For all that rugged performance, however, they require a little tender loving care, as do all cast-iron pans. First, you'll need to cure or season your Dutch oven or pan before you use it for the first time and then occasionally thereafter. Here's what I recommend you do each time you put a new cast-iron piece into service.

1. Wash the pan or pot and lid with mild soapy water to remove any residue from the manufacturing process, rinse them, and dry them with a cloth or paper towel; then set aside to dry thoroughly.

2. While your Dutch oven is drying, take all the racks out of your kitchen oven except the bottom two and cover the very bottom rack with aluminum foil. Preheat your oven to 350°F (177°C).

3. Coat the Dutch oven and lid with vegetable oil, making sure both the inner and outer surfaces are coated. I usually use a cooking oil spray. Turn the Dutch oven upside down and place it and the lid in your oven. Depending on the size of your oven, you may need to lean the lid against the Dutch oven rather than lay it flat during heating. Now set your timer to 60 minutes.

Welded wheel rims make great Dutch-oven stands.

4. When the timer buzzes, turn off the oven and let the pan or pot and lid sit in the oven for an hour or two or overnight so they can cool down.

5. When they're cool enough to handle, pull them out of the oven and wipe them down with paper towels or a cloth to remove any excess vegetable oil. I'd leave them out for another few hours on your counter so the oil dries out and fully saturates the pores in the metal.

Each time I buy a new Dutch oven I also purchase a nice fabric case, which protects the pot and provides a means to carry and store it. Store your Dutch oven in a dry spot when not in use so it doesn't become subject to moisture that can cause rust to form. I place a paper towel between the lid and the pan to protect them from rusting.

CLEANING. It's important to clean your Dutch oven and lid after every use so you can count on years and years of good performance. Simply rinse them with water; don't use any dishwashing liquid, which can damage the seasoned surface. If there's food stuck on the inside, you may need to boil some water in the pot to loosen it up. Don't scrape the sides or lid since that can damage the surface. Try using a sponge or plastic scrubber to remove any remaining food. Rinse the pot well, dry it with a towel, and then allow it to air-dry thoroughly before you put it back in the case. After a few uses and cleanings you may feel the Dutch oven and lid need seasoning again. Simply repeat the instructions above.

There are a number of Dutch oven manufacturers around that you can try. I've had my best experience with products from Lodge. They are of high quality and hold up well. You'll find numerous sizes to fit your needs. Give Dutch-oven cooking a serious try—you'll have fun and really enjoy the results.

We've covered several cooking options in this chapter. If you have a gas or charcoal grill, next up—add a butane stove for cooking indoors. When your budget allows, consider an outdoor oven for baking. Maybe those three devices are all you need and want, or maybe you'll want to increase your cooking options as I've done. Isn't it a relief to know that in an emergency power outage you don't have to subsist on canned beans and water? That you can cook a meal and make hot cocoa or a cup of tea? Perhaps after reading this chapter, you'll want to revisit your food storage plan and add in some meals and foods you didn't think you'd have the resources to prepare. I hope you feel more comfortable with planning and preparing for how you'll cook during an emergency and that you will be more comfortable in any emergency situation.

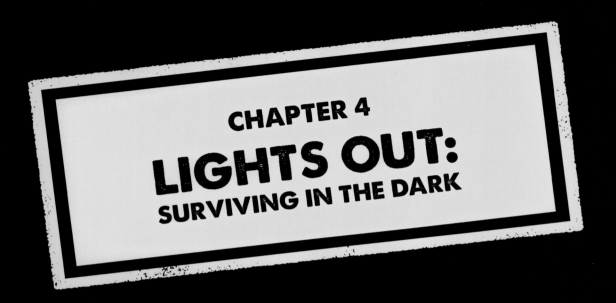

CHAPTER 4
LIGHTS OUT:
SURVIVING IN THE DARK

You hear an explosion and instantly the power in your home is lost. A local transformer has blown, and it's lights out... and TV out, fridge out, heat out.... Do you have what it takes to shed some light and heat on the situation?

In this chapter, you'll learn the different types of lighting you can use to light your home in the dark, how to keep warm when your main source of heat is gone, and how to keep cool in the heat without a functioning air conditioner. We'll also go over your options for generators and how to get news on the outside world. In the next power outage, you'll be confident that your family can bunker down safely and comfortably.

The lights go out, the TV screen goes dark, the numbers on your digital clock disappear—signs of a power outage. And when the electricity doesn't pop back on after a few minutes as it sometimes does when there's a power interruption, you look across the street to see if your neighbors' lights are out. And then you peer down the street to see if the whole neighborhood is affected and when you realize it is, you check the news on your cell phone or call some friends and you learn that the power lines are down and there's no estimate as to when power will be restored.

Well, you won't be watching your favorite television show tonight. And then it occurs to you that you won't be cooking dinner on your electric stove or in the microwave. Forget about that load of laundry you had planned to wash. But the power will come back on soon, you say to yourself optimistically. You go to bed hoping that by the morning everything will be back to normal.

Day two: You wake up and power has not returned. You realize you can't use your cordless phone because it needs electricity, and your cell phone is running low on battery, so you charge it in your car. You check in with neighbors to see if they are okay and if anyone needs anything or knows anything new about the outage, and you learn that local officials don't know when power will be restored. You may be without it for a while.

Power outages happen in the day, they happen in the night, and they happen more often with the increasing frequency of severe weather that we're experiencing across the country. Most likely, you won't have any warning, or if your community learns that a big storm is headed your way, batteries and flashlights will become as scarce as bread and milk. It's best to plan ahead and store some items that you'll need or want in an emergency power outage.

You can buy a whole-house generator to take care of your energy needs, but these are very expensive, and they run on gasoline, so you'll need to store several gallons on your property, which is something I am not very comfortable doing. And then once you've used up all of your fuel, you'll need to use other means of getting by without power. I've done a lot of research into solar-powered generators and learned that most will not meet the needs of my refrigerator or other appliances that require a lot of energy, but they can be handy for items that don't run on a lot of watts. Let's take a look at some of the little things you can do that will make a big difference during a power outage.

SEEING IN THE DARK

Sure you'll miss many of your electric-powered appliances and gadgets but what's most important is to see well enough to function in your home. You will need some sort of emergency lighting. Check these out.

FLASHLIGHTS

Everyone in your family should have a flashlight for safety.

Fortunately many cell phones these days have a built-in flashlight function so that you have immediate access to light if, like most people, you have your phone with you at all times. However, the phone's flashlight is not likely to be very powerful and in an emergency, you will want to conserve your phone's battery life for making calls or sending messages. Therefore, I recommend that you store battery-powered flashlights as part of your emergency plan.

Every member in your household should have a battery-powered flashlight that's kept near their bed at night. It should be the size you can hold in your hand and hopefully can also fit in your pocket, about 5-7 inches (13-18 cm) long and 1 inch (3 cm) in diameter. Make sure you have a good supply of batteries and store them in a cool, dry place. If you use your flashlight infrequently, check it every few months to make sure the batteries are still working well, and replace them if light is dim. I like flashlights that you crank by hand since they don't rely on batteries for power. My absolute favorite, though, are flashlights that you can charge with a hand crank or through their built-in solar panels. The Goal Zero flashlight I have can last up to 48 hours before I need to recharge it. No batteries needed.

Pros: They turn on instantly with the turn of a switch or button. Some flashlights you can crank by hand for more light, charge in your car, or use solar power to recharge them. The battery-powered ones are typically inexpensive.

Cons: Some need batteries and once the batteries are gone, you have zero light. The flashlights that require zero batteries are typically more expensive than the battery-powered ones.

HEADLAMPS

The idea of wearing a headlamp may seem strange, but it's very practical. I suggest you consider buying some for your family to use during a power outage. You'll find it so gratifying not to have to carry a flashlight, candle, or lantern as you move around your house and to have your hands free to do whatever you need to do. And headlamps put out a decent amount of light. I learned to use them in my Community Emergency Response Team (C.E.R.T.) class. They come in a wide range of prices from very inexpensive to very expensive. What kid wouldn't love to wear one of these headlamps? I know my grandkids would want them if the power goes out. The only downside is that they use batteries. I live in southern Utah and I can't store more than six months' worth of batteries because they go bad very quickly. This is why I'm not a fan of products that require batteries.

Pros: Fairly inexpensive, and you can see where you are working in the dark.

Cons: If you run out of batteries they will not work. Also, you may get tired of wearing a headlamp every night.

CANDLES

For centuries candles were used to light homes. They are an effective way to light individual rooms, and there's something nostalgically romantic about the old-world feel of a candlelit home. They come in a variety of sizes, and the large ones will burn for a long time. But you need to very careful about placing them in a sturdy holder and away from anything flammable. I wouldn't leave a small child alone in a room with candles.

Pros: Fairly inexpensive in most cases.

Cons: They are an open flame and you should not use them in a room where oxygen is being used because it's flammable. Never leave a room with a lit candle burning. They also do not put out enough light unless several are burning in one room. Matches would be necessary to have with them or they would be useless.

GLOW STICKS

These are the little units that you snap or shake to activate. They'll give you a little bit of light from minutes to hours and can be used in a pinch. I remember seeing kids carrying these on Halloween. Well, glow sticks have come a long way, baby. Yes, you can buy them at the dollar store, but you can purchase military- or industrial-strength glow sticks that will last much longer. Are they safe? Yes... and no. You don't want little kids swallowing pieces of the glow stick if it should break or ingesting the whole thing. The liquid is not for human consumption. It's recommended that you not give glow sticks to children under 5. If you're wondering how they work, when you snap or shake the stick, it mixes the substances inside the stick to create a chemical reaction that produces the glow. Here's what's inside:

- ☐ 4 g sodium carbonate
- ☐ 0.2 g luminol
- ☐ 0.5 g ammonium carbonate
- ☐ 0.4 g copper sulfate pentahydrate
- ☐ Approximately 1 L of distilled water
- ☐ 50 ml of 3% hydrogen peroxide

You'll find an expiration date on most packs of glow sticks. Be sure to store them in a cool, dry place.

Pros: Inexpensive and waterproof.

Cons: Small children under 5 shouldn't use the glow sticks. They will not light up a room. They only burn from 4-12 hours depending on the brand you purchase.

LANTERNS

Our ancestors relied on lanterns as a light source for decades and they've come a long way thanks to technology. You can still find and use oil lamps and the old camping lanterns my family used when I was a young girl. I don't recommend using liquid fuel lanterns indoors, but they would be fine outdoors.

I lean toward solar lamps because I expect that when night falls, I'll be spending more time inside my house then. I charge them in my wall outlets and they are ready when the power goes out. I can also charge them in my car and outside using the solar panels. My favorite is the Goal Zero Lighthouse 250. It doesn't require batteries, can be charged with a USB connection, solar panel, or a hand crank—no other fuel required. And the charge will last up to 48 hours and that's a long time if you think about it. You won't need to use the lantern during the day, only at night when it's dark. I may use the lantern for only 4 hours a night, which means this lantern could last me 12 days without having to be recharged. Awesome!

Another lamp I like is the Sun Bell Solar Lamp and Phone Charger. It is fairly inexpensive and will light a room for 4.5 to 136 hours depending on whether you use it on low, medium, or high output. And depending on sunlight conditions, it will recharge in 3 to 10 hours with its solar panel. You can hang it from the ceiling to light up a small room. You can hang it around your neck while walking or use the handle to carry it while travelling or walking room to room. Bonus—it has a USB phone charger. Gotta love it!

If your preference is for the cozy, romantic glow of an oil lamp, these, too, have come a long way. Kerosene and other liquid fuels were commonly used to light oil lamps, but they were messy and stunk up the house. Newer products, such as Kleanheat and Aladdin oil, available from Lehman's, are two fuels that burn smoke- and odor-free and can be safely stored and used indoors (note: don't ever mix fuels). Kleanheat has a shelf life of five years and Aladdin oil will last indefinitely.

Then there's the time-honored, traditional Coleman lantern. This company makes a variety of models. You'll find lanterns that work off kerosene, unleaded gasoline, Coleman liquid fuel, or batteries. One model uses a propane tank and lasts nearly 14 hours on one 16.4-pound (62-L) cylinder of propane. Only the battery-powered lantern is safe to use indoors but the others are great for camping if you have the space to store the fuel.

Pros: You can light up a room with the indoor units. You can charge some units in your car. Just turn the button or switch on the lantern and they turn on instantly. Some units can charge your cell phone because they have a USB connection.

Cons: Some units must be used only outdoors, so check with the manufacturer. Fuel needs to be stored for some of the lanterns. Solar units need the sun to recharge. Some units are more expensive. Some lanterns require batteries—once the battery goes, so does the lantern.

OUTDOOR SOLAR LAMPS

If you use solar lamps outdoors as accent lights for landscaping or to light walkways or patios, you can bring them in at night to help light your home. The only drawback is the hassle of moving them in and out of your house, and they won't be a very reliable source of light if you live in an area with limited daily sunshine.

Pros: Inexpensive and you may have them in your yard already.

Cons: You need to take the lights outside to recharge them when needed, usually every day since they do not last that long.

EATING IN

If you've read Chapter 3, you can take comfort in knowing that you don't need electricity to cook your food or heat water, and that there are a variety of excellent nonelectric cooking appliances to choose from, including the butane stove, which you can use indoors. No stove or oven? No problem. But your refrigerator and freezer require electricity and lots of it. With a large enough generator and a steady supply of gasoline for that generator, you'd be able to keep running your refrigerator. Without one, you'll want to make every effort to keep the air inside as cool as possible for as long as possible by opening the doors only when absolutely necessary. If your refrigerator or freezer is full when the power goes out, the food should last a day or two, depending on the temperature inside your house.

When it appears that you're going to be without power for an extended period of time and you know the food in your fridge or freezer is going to spoil, it's time to throw that neighborhood barbecue you've been contemplating but haven't gotten around to organizing. Cook all your meat, eggs, and any vegetables that you won't be able to save.

Another option is to can your foods if you have a stove that can handle your pressure canner. The older style electric stoves with the circular heating elements on top can generally handle pressure canning foods, depending on the temperatures needed by the canner and the length of time for the process to work. Most serious canners will invest in a gas stove since they seem to be better designed to handle the higher temperatures and the weight for longer periods, and the gas controls are more efficient since they have "immediate heat/immediate off" flame control. Check your electric glass-top stove manufacturer's handbook, because in some states they do not recommend them for water bath canning or pressure canning foods. My All American Pressure canner weighs over 25 pounds (11.3 kg) empty. The weight would be much more with filled jars and water inside of it. You could crack your glass stove top with excessive weight if it cannot handle while canning. I used to "can" outside on a propane stove until I was able to replace my glass-top stove for a gas stove. Plus, if the heat gets too high, the stove may automatically lower the temperature and you may not be able to safely can your food. Again, check with your stove's manufacturer to see if your stove is acceptable to use for water bath canning or pressure canning. If you contact your manufacturer, state the weight of your pressure canner. Ask if you can water bath or pressure can your foods. There is a big difference in the safety of canning between the two types of procedures.

WARMING UP, COOLING OFF

Depending on where you live, the season, and the weather, it might be frightfully cold or sweltering hot outside, which means the inside of your house is going to get chilly or toasty. With no electricity to power your heating system or air-conditioning, you'll want to store some simple items that can help warm you up or cool you down. If you have a solar generator that you've kept charged, you should be fine to run some fans or small space heaters, but I recommend conserving as much of that solar power as possible for energy needs that are more crucial. Use these simple tips to try to get comfortable before you tap into your generator.

STAYING WARM

I have one word for you—blankets. You can layer them on top of you to stay warm as the temperature inside your home drops. Never give away blankets unless they are totally worn out and buy some inexpensive ones to store. I look for sales on quilts as winter comes to a close, and if I see a great deal, I'll pick up a few and add them to my stash. They seem to be warmer than the comforters I've bought in the past. Of course, they're not too practical to use when you need to move around the house or go outside to use the grill, so store extra jackets, hats, mittens, gloves, and scarves. My husband and I moved to southern Utah to escape the snow up north but we still keep our jackets in case we're visiting some place where it's cold and they've proven handy during power outages. If you're in the market for extra winter clothing and accessories, garage sales and thrift stores are terrific options for purchasing cold-weather wear and blankets at great prices. You might also consider having on hand some long underwear, available now in a variety of fabrics that are light in weight and comfortable to wear while providing an extra layer of warmth when temperatures drop.

When my husband was a volunteer for the 2002 Winter Olympics in Salt Lake City, he was given a supply of hand warmers to use during the evening practices for both the opening and closing ceremonies. You may have heard of the brand HotHands. These are small air-activated heat packs. You simply open the package, shake it, and put it inside your glove, mitten, or pocket to keep your hand warm. We used the leftover hand warmers for winter outings, and on many a night, we were very grateful to have them. They are handy when shoveling snow, skiing, tubing, camping, or enjoying any other winter activity, and you'll be glad you have them if your power goes out during cold weather. Though they're called hand warmers, they can be used inside your socks to keep your feet warm, too.

Use hand warmers to help your hands and feet stay warm in cold conditions—such as a power outage in winter.

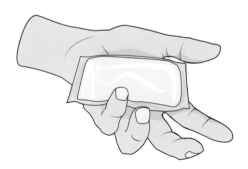

Heat in a can uses supplies most families already have.

Don't make these up to store indoors—they are too flammable.

Use caution when lighting these units. Have the kids stand back.

Even better than hand warmers, according to my friends Wally and Danielle, who are avid hunters, is heat in a can. This is a simple little makeshift heater for use outdoors. To make one you'll need the following supplies:

☐   A clean quart-size paint can with a lid

☐   A roll of toilet paper

☐   A bottle of 70 to 90 percent rubbing alcohol

☐   Matches

☐   A can opener

Roll the toilet paper between your hands to loosen up the inner cardboard tube. Remove the tube and put the toilet paper in the paint can. Add enough alcohol to saturate the paper and then light it with a match. Use the lid to snuff out the flame. (See the illustrations for visual step-by-step instructions.)

WARMING UP YOUR HOME. If you have a fireplace you'll need to consider whether it will help heat the room or if it's going to draw air out and up the chimney, which many fireplaces will do. A true heating fireplace needs to have a shallow depth. A fireplace insert or wood-burning stove, however, can be very effective for heating a room. Pellet stoves and gas fireplaces have become very popular and are very effective heat sources during cold seasons, but both require electricity to run and won't be of any use to you in a power outage. If you are serious about investing in a wood-burning source of heat, which will not only help keep you warm in an emergency but can reduce oil, gas, or electric heating bills during winter months, look at stoves and inserts. Of course, you have the option of plugging an electric heater into a generator, but it will use a lot of power, so you wouldn't want to run it nonstop. I am a big believer in the warming power of clothes and blankets. Wrap up in them and gather together in a room in your house—bodies are an excellent source of warmth, too.

Heater or no heater, fireplace or no fireplace, designate one room in your home where your entire family can gather. Close the doors and hang blankets over windows if needed to prevent cool air from penetrating, and get cozy together. I remember a time when my four daughters were little that we all gathered on my king-size bed to watch a movie and dine on buttered popcorn. Maybe a movie won't be an option but you can read a book out loud, play cards, or just have a conversation. You can find ways to create good times in bad situations.

PREP YOUR HOUSE FOR THE COLD. Each year your family should do a house inspection for energy efficiency. If you can see sunlight coming into any room from under or around any exterior doors, it is time to install or replace the weather stripping and/or door thresholds. Also look for any cracks in the framing around your doors and windows where cold air could seep in and patch them. Many old homes could use additional insulation in the attic to help conserve both warm air in the winter and cooler air-conditioned air in the summer. If your home still has single-pane windows, consider saving up to replace those windows with more energy-efficient double- or triple-pane windows. Whether or not you ever have a power outage, you'll be grateful for the energy efficiency these windows provide and your lower monthly energy bills.

GETTING COOL

When your air conditioner stops running, open some windows and doors in your house to create cross ventilation, unless it is very hot outside or the air quality is poor. I look forward to the time early each year when I can open doors in the front and back of my house so a breeze can flow through. On those superhot days, it's a good idea to cover windows to help shield the interior of your home from glaring sun. I have shutters on the windows that face the sun and they really make a difference in the temperature inside my home. We also had some special screens installed that are designed to block the UV rays from hitting the glass and raising the heat inside the house. They are attached to the outside window frame but can be removed easily with the slight twist of some brackets. They block up to 90 percent of the sun's rays, which is the primary cause of heat in homes during the summer months, and I can open the windows with the screens in place. Awnings also help but can be pretty expensive.

SQUIRT BOTTLES ARE A MUST. Think about how your body cools itself naturally—you sweat and the evaporation of that moisture from your skin creates cooling. By squirting water on your skin and clothes, you are facilitating that same cooling process. I suggest buying a squirt bottle for everyone in your house. Some have a battery-powered fan, and they're great to have on hand for those especially hot times of day. Try to use them infrequently though to preserve battery life.

It's important to stay cool if you live in a hot climate and your air-conditioning stops working during an emergency. Cooling towels like Frogg Toggs work great.

USE A COOLING TOWEL. Try this on to keep cool—a cooling towel. Here in southern Utah, the temperature can climb up to between 110 and 120°F (43-49°C) in the summer. I'd been looking for anything to help survive the heat when a salesclerk at a store where I was shopping suggested a Frogg Toggs Chilly Pad Towel. I usually don't fall for sales pitches but I did that day, and I'm glad. This towel is amazing. It's made of a synthetic hyper-evaporative material that absorbs a ton of water yet feels dry to the touch. When you wet it—with either warm or cool water—it instantly feels cooler. Simply hang the towel around your neck, and you'll feel cooler, too. When it dries, it becomes stiff. Simply rewet it, and let the cooling begin again. It comes 33 inches (84 cm) by 13 inches (33 cm), but you can cut it in smaller pieces if needed for your kids. There's also a smaller sport version. The Chilly Towel is designed to last for years and is machine washable. So when the heat is on throw one of these wet babies around your neck. I promise you will be amazed at how comfortable you'll feel on a really hot day.

WEAR SOME COOL CLOTHES. And I'm not talking about the latest fashion trends, you won't care about that when you're sweating buckets, I'm talking about technical fabrics that help wick away moisture from your skin. Cotton is a lovely warm-weather fabric but when it gets soaked with sweat, it stays soaked and sticks to your skin, making you very uncomfortable and warm. There are several brands of synthetic fabrics today made from fibers that pull the water away from your skin and up to the surface of the clothing where it evaporates and keeps you cooler. Athletes and sports enthusiasts wear this type of apparel pretty much exclusively during warm months.

TAKE A DIP. If there's a swimming lake nearby or stream, you can cool off in the water. We have a pool in our yard and we love it, especially on days when the temperature soars, but if the electricity isn't working and the water isn't circulating as designed, the pool may become a haven for bacteria. You can also take showers to help cool off when the heat gets too unbearable, or better yet, fill your tub with cool water and each family member can take short dips in the water. Sure, the water will gradually get warmer until it reaches room temperature, but it will still feel cooler than the hot air in your home or apartment.

You can help everyone in your family get through a power outage more comfortably by planning for one and talking about it ahead of time. Discuss everyone's wants and needs, understanding that we each have different priorities while also preparing your teens to do without some of those "necessities" like hair dryers and curling irons that draw much too much wattage. If you do have a generator, you want to decide in advance how and when you'll use that precious energy resource. Finally, review with everyone what to do if the power goes out, and give each of your kids a flashlight and help them find a spot near their bed to store it. Preparing not only your home but your family for a power outage will go a long way in making it as comfortable as it can be should one occur and maybe even a little fun.

POWER GENERATORS

In the book I mention the use of generators when the power goes out. I also mention that full-house power generators aren't practical for most families due to cost, fuel storage concerns, space availability, maintenance issues, and other issues. I base most of my power generation solutions on Goal Zero products like the Yeti 400 and Yeti 1250, and these are my top recommendations for generators. You can run commonly used appliances like mixers, wheat grinders, fans, computers, small TVs, and the like. They can also be lifesavers in a power outage if you require a medical device that runs on electricity. They are easy to use and can be recharged by plugging them in when the power is restored or through the solar panels that are easily set up in a yard.

I realize that some families may want to get more serious about power generation and have a system in place that will run the majority of their household needs, including a furnace and air conditioner. I will outline some important issues to consider as you perform your own research in this regard.

Power generators come in many varieties—those that are portable and those that are permanently installed and are called "stationary" or "standby." Both types can generally run on a wide range of fuels like gasoline, propane, natural gas, and diesel. Although the portable units are cheaper and require an investment in hundreds of dollars, depending on the generation capacity, they also have their own set of challenges to consider facing when the emergency requires their use. Since they are portable they need to be stored somewhere on your property where they can be accessed, transported to the location for use, fueled up, manually started, and monitored. Since they are smaller and portable, the fuel tanks connected to them also are smaller and need to be refilled more often. Size also relates to the power output they generate, so when connecting them to the power panel designed for their use they usually are connected to the more critical or desirable circuits rather than the full-house electrical panel.

Those kitchen appliances can "come to life" when the power goes out if you have steady power from a properly charged generator.

One key advantage with some portable units is that if your home is the only one in the neighborhood without power and your portable generator can run on an external source provided by a neighbor close by, you can take advantage of that source and run the unit for longer periods than trying to use the small tank provided with the unit. An example of this is if you have enough tubing you could possibly connect your unit to a neighbor's propane tank, neighbor willing. When considering a portable unit for power generation it would be wise to get one slightly larger than what you think you'll need rather than a small capacity one and then be disappointed when you run short of power just when you need it. When using portable units for temporary power generation I'd certainly look at one that generates 3,000- to 8,000-watt units. Some of the quality manufacturers of portable generators are Briggs & Stratton, Generac, Champion, Honda, Yamaha, Subaru, Kohler, and DeWalt.

One of the key factors for considering a more costly standby generator is convenience. Since they are left in place they are permanently connected to your home's electrical panel and are the fuel source to be used to run the unit. I'd certainly suggest you also spend some additional dollars to get a unit that includes automatic systems that immediately recognize that power has been lost and transfers the power over to the generator from the house power. This can all take place when you are away from your home, thus protecting food in the refrigerator and/or freezer, protecting house plants and pets from getting too hot or cold, and keeping your alarm system and other critical operations running in your absence. The tendency may be to strongly consider using natural gas to run your standby generator since it is already available on your property, costs less than most other fuels, and has fewer emissions and smells when being burned. I would caution you to think twice if you live in an earthquake-prone area since natural gas lines often break in an earthquake, thus leaving you with a fancy generator that can't run due to lack of available fuel. Also make sure your installer validates the capacity of the natural gas meter servicing your home. You may have the extra expense of putting in a larger meter to properly supply sufficient natural gas to run the generator. Some generators minimize this issue by being constructed such that they can use both natural gas or propane once some adjustments are made to the unit. Gasoline and diesel present other issues like the safety of storage, the fuels can go "bad" over time, and have to be replaced or treated to bring them back into burnable condition.

Depending on what is plugged in and running in your home you will probably need somewhere between a 15 kW to 25 kW unit. Of course, the higher the capacity the more costly. I wouldn't base your decision mainly on cost. Once the decision to go with a standby unit is made, spend enough to be satisfied with the power and convenience you want.

Some additional things to consider are the cost of getting the necessary permits your community or utility company may require and hiring competent licensed contractors (which could require both electrical and plumbing expertise). Also you may want to consider a support platform made of cement to provide the stability needed for the heavy units involved. Manufacturers to consider for this type of power generation are Kohler, Generac, Briggs & Stratton, and others your contractor might suggest based on projected wattage needed and your budget.

KITCHEN GADGETS

Perhaps the most important gadget in a power outage is a can opener. Make sure you have two or three manual openers because the electric one will be down and there's no need to waste any generator power running a can opener. You will need a sizable generator to use your toaster or blender—these appliances use 1,800 watts or more. My Goal Zero solar-powered generators (depending on the watts) can drive some of my small kitchen appliances, such as these:

- ☐ Bosch bread mixer: 800 watts
- ☐ KitchenAid Stand Mixer—6 quart model: 575 watts
- ☐ L'Equip NutriMill Wheat Grinder: 1200 watts
- ☐ Fagor Pressure Cooker: 1000 watts
- ☐ Cuisinart Rice Cooker: 650 watts
- ☐ Villa Maker Waffle Maker: 1000 watts
- ☐ Portable electric fan: 27 watts

YOU COULD ALSO USE A SOLAR GENERATOR TO POWER THESE ITEMS:

- ☐ Lamp: 60 watts
- ☐ CPAP Sleep Apnea Machine (my son-in-law's): 90 watts (he was able to use the Goal Zero YETI 400 for 8 ½ hours to sleep overnight)
- ☐ Nebulizer: 300 watts (my Goal Zero YETI 400 worked great with my adopted granddaughter's nebulizer)
- ☐ My Parabolic portable space heater: 1000 watts (but uses way too much power in a very short time)
- ☐ 32-inch (81-cm) Television with DVD: works with Goal Zero YETI 400

I cannot use my solar generators to power my Cuisinart toaster (1800 watts), VitaMix blender (1380 watts), or BlendTec blender (1560 watts). I crisp up my bread on the grill and simply do without smoothies until electricity is restored.

STORE THIS ADVICE

If you take medications that need to be refrigerated, consider buying a small refrigerator like those used on boats that you can plug into your car, run on a stand-alone battery, or that uses solar power.

KEEPING IN CONTACT

You must have contact with the outside world in any power outage so that you know whether to stay in your home or leave and also to try to learn how long you'll be without electricity so you can figure out how far you may need to stretch your food and water supplies. And, you'll want to stay in touch with friends and family members as well as have the capability of making a call for emergency medical services or the fire department.

Most families have cell phones, but they regularly need to be recharged. Purchase a phone charger to work with your car, and look into solar cell phone chargers, which work best of course on a bright sunny day. Neither option is foolproof, which is why you might want to consider getting an old-fashioned landline phone that plugs into the phone jack in your home and doesn't rely on electricity to function. They're very inexpensive, although if you use only your cell phone to cut costs as many families do these days, you'll be adding back those costs with a home phone line.

With no television or radio, you can use any number of free news apps on your smartphone to stay abreast of the news and what's happening locally, statewide, or nationally, but again, keeping one charged for days or weeks could be challenging. Look into getting a hand-cranked radio designed for emergencies and put your own power to use to charge it up. Some come with solar panels and even allow you to charge your cell phone.

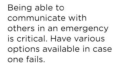

Being able to communicate with others in an emergency is critical. Have various options available in case one fails.

A MEDICAL NECESSITY

If anyone in your family needs a nebulizer, CPAP, or other medical equipment, you'll need to get a generator to have on hand for emergency power outages. I highly recommend Goal Zero solar generators. You will need to check the wattage requirements of your medical equipment and purchase the unit that matches that wattage. My son-in-law needs to use a CPAP, which requires about 80 watts of power. I had him try my Goal Zero YETI 400 one night for 8 hours and it worked perfectly. He had power to spare. He now keeps the generator charged via the wall outlet and If the power goes out, he can take the solar panels outside where, they'll collect energy from the sun to charge the YETI for another night or two of sleep.

A TV AND DVD?

I am a huge advocate for reserving generators—if you have one—for true energy necessities so it may seem odd that I'm making a case for powering a television and DVD player, but my niece Maralee, who lives in New Jersey and experienced Hurricane Sandy with her family, shared this story with me: "After Hurricane Sandy, we were out of power for five days. We had a generator, but it was not enough to run our heater, so we debated what to use it for. Eventually we plugged the TV and PlayStation into it and let the boys play for the sake of morale. The temperatures outside were in the mid-50's so we weren't in dire straits when it came to needing our heat, but it set off a discussion for the future, which was good because the following winter we lost power several times as a result of ice storms." Maralee went on to say that their family was so glad they had made that decision since having two very active boys at home with nothing to do for days at a time would have been an additional challenge. They sat by the fireplace, which now has an insert, huddled in blankets, eating popcorn and watching movies. Maralee said it helped reduce stress by taking the outside world out of the picture for a few hours each day.

CHAPTER 5

FIRST AID:
MEDICAL PREPAREDNESS

In the event of a major disaster, all doctors, nurses, and paramedics will be called into action. No one will be available to come to you if you are injured or sick. Make first aid a priority in your family. It might save the life of someone you love.

In this chapter, you'll assemble a first-aid kit that will meet the basic medical needs of your family in a number of situations. You'll learn what you need for a general first-aid kit and children's first-aid kit. I'll also share with you my favorite home remedies using common household items to relieve a variety of issues.

We've all faced times when someone we are close to gets sick or hurt. A decision needs to be made as to whether a trip to the doctor, an emergency clinic, or the ER is necessary or if the injury or illness can be treated at home. None of us wants to be placed in a situation where our actions can mean the difference between life and death, but that choice may not be ours to make. You may be the first responder when your child falls and is bleeding profusely from a deep wound or your husband burns his hand while cooking over an open fire in the backyard or your elderly neighbor collapses in the heat. If you are the first person to come to someone's aid in a medical emergency, I'm sure you would rather be prepared not only with the right first-aid supplies but also with knowing how to use them and what to do.

First aid seems to be a catchall for a number of things. It may mean providing fairly simple care if someone is sick or hurt such as reducing a high fever, bandaging a wound, helping to hydrate, and cooling someone showing signs of heat illness. It may mean stabilizing someone until EMTs arrive or until you can get that person to a care facility or hospital. And it may also mean administering CPR or applying a defibrillator to save a life on the spot.

I think it is vital that each of us, and particularly parents of young children and caregivers of the elderly, sign up for first-aid training. The American Red Cross offers a variety of classes across the country in adult and/or pediatric first aid, CPR, and AED. Visit their website where you can do a simple search that will bring up several options near where you live. Your local police and fire departments or YMCA may also offer classes. And in the meantime, put together a well-stocked first-aid kit for your home as well as one for your car.

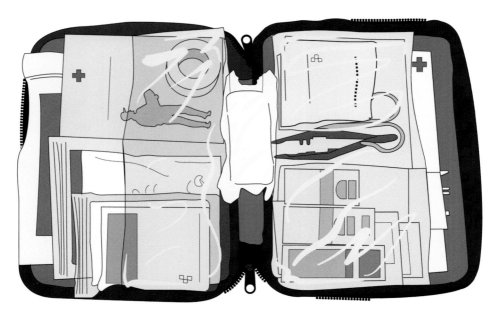

Having a quality first-aid kit and the knowledge of how to use all the contents is an important part of your emergency-preparedness plan.

GENERAL FIRST-AID KIT

As you'll see later, I recommend creating a kit that specifically address the needs of your children or grandchildren, especially since over-the-counter medications are age specific, but begin by putting together a basic first-aid kit because most of those supplies will be needed to treat an injury or illness in both children and adults. The following is a list of items that the Red Cross recommends for a family of four:

- ☐ Absorbent compress dressings, 5 x 9 inches (13-23 cm), 2
- ☐ Adhesive bandages (commonly referred to as Band-Aids), 25 in assorted sizes
- ☐ Adhesive cloth tape, 1 (10-yd [9-M]) roll of 1-inch (3-cm) tape
- ☐ Antibiotic ointment, 5 packets, approximately 1 gram each
- ☐ Antiseptic wipe packets, 5
- ☐ Aspirin, 2 packets of 81 milligram tablets, commonly called baby aspirin and used in case of a heart attack
- ☐ Bandages
- ☐ 3-inch (8-cm) wide roller bandage, 1
- ☐ 4-inch (10-cm) wide roller bandage, 1
- ☐ Triangular bandages, 2

- ☐ Breathing barrier with one-way valve, 1
- ☐ First-aid instruction booklet (you can purchase one from the Red Cross)
- ☐ Hydrocortisone ointment, 2 packets, approximately 1 gram each
- ☐ Instant cold compress, 1
- ☐ No latex gloves, large, 2 pairs
- ☐ Scissors for cutting bandages, trimming gauze pads, and other needs
- ☐ Space blanket, 1
- ☐ Sterile gauze pads, 3 x 3 inches (8 x 8 cm), 5
- ☐ Sterile gauze pads, 4 x 4 inches (10 x 10 cm), 5
- ☐ Thermometer, non-mercury
- ☐ Tweezers

STORE THIS ADVICE

- ☐ Regularly check the expiration dates on all first-aid ointments and over-the-counter products that will lose their potency after a period of time and replace them as needed.

- ☐ Aim to have on hand at least an extra month's supply of contact lenses and cleaning solution (or an extra pair of glasses), sunscreen, birth control, whatever personal items you use on a regular basis.

YOUR MUST-HAVE MEDICATIONS

Going without a prescription medication can be devastating to your health if not deadly. Ask your doctor if he or she would be willing to give you a prescription for an extra month or two, just in case. Even medications for mental health should be considered in your emergency-preparedness supplies if a family member needs them. And if you have a pet that requires regular meds, ask for extras for him or her, too.

ADDITIONAL ITEMS TO CONSIDER

I like having several other supplies around so that I am prepared to treat blisters, colds, splinters, and a wide range of minor ills that generally don't fall under the category of first aid. In addition to the basics above, I recommend storing the following items:

- ☐ Antifungal ointment
- ☐ Antidiarrhea medication, such as Imodium
- ☐ Anti-inflammatories for headache and other pain relief, acetaminophen (Tylenol), ibuprofen (Advil, Motrin), or naproxen (Aleve)
- ☐ Benzocaine topical ointment, common brand Orajel
- ☐ Blister treatment medication and pads
- ☐ Calamine lotion
- ☐ Castor oil
- ☐ Cough medicine such as Mucinex or Mucinex Dm
- ☐ Ear-loop masks (N-95)
- ☐ Eye patch
- ☐ Hand sanitizer
- ☐ Heating pads
- ☐ Insect repellant, 100% DEET
- ☐ Hemorrhoid cream or pads
- ☐ Hydrocortisone
- ☐ Knife
- ☐ Liquid bandage such as New Skin
- ☐ Magnifying glass
- ☐ Molefoam or Moleskin pads
- ☐ Monistat or other antifungal cream to treat yeast Infections

- ☐ Motion sickness medication such as Dramamine
- ☐ Nail clippers
- ☐ Nasal decongestant
- ☐ Nasal spray
- ☐ Neti pot nasal irrigation
- ☐ Nystatin and Triamcinolone Acetonide
- ☐ Petroleum jelly
- ☐ Pepto-Bismol Chewables
- ☐ Peroxide
- ☐ Splinter removal kit
- ☐ Splints, large and small
- ☐ Sterile water

Who would have thought that a fishing tackle box could become such an efficient first-aid kit?

Make sure you have a first-aid kit ready to go that will fit the needs of the kids in your home.

CHILDREN'S FIRST-AID KIT

Kids' needs are different from adults' and most medications, over-the-counter or otherwise, must be dosed according to a child's age and size. For these reasons, I put together a kit using a small plastic container that I filled with child-appropriate first-aid supplies and other child-care items that I want to have readily available when the grandkids come to visit. I don't want my daughters to have to look all over the house if they need to treat a headache, cough, splinter, burn, or other minor ill or injury. I also don't want them to be using adult-strength medications. Customize your kit to the ages of your children or grandchildren. Here are the items I recommend:

☐ **Adhesive bandages** (better known as Band-Aids) decorated with colorful designs or animated movie characters. Kids love them, and a little fun helps make the pain go away.

☐ **Anti-inflammatories** for reducing fever. Acetaminophen (Tylenol) or ibuprofen (Advil or Motrin) are available in infant and children's formulas. Note: aspirin is not recommend for anyone under 18.

☐ **Antibiotic ointment** (such as Neosporin or Polysporin). You'll have this in your general first-aid kit, but I'd include it in your kid kit as well, since it seems girls and boys get scrapes and cuts all the time.

☐ **Baby lotion, shampoo, and sunscreen.** Young children need gentle care for tender skin and scalp.

☐ **Baby wipes.** Even if you don't have an infant, these wipes come in handy for cleaning sticky fingers, and you can even use them to wipe the paws of a pet who's been outside in the rain or mud.

☐ **Benzocaine topical ointment** (such as Orajel). This can help with teething pain.

☐ **Bulb syringe** to clear mucous from the nose for easier breathing.

☐ **Diaper rash cream.** This stuff will quickly clear up a rash on your baby's bottom and may come in handy to relieve irritation from diarrhea. It can also help relieve other skin rashes. Be sure to consult the manufacturer's directions for use.

☐ **Diaper pins.** Necessary for cloth diapers, these can also be used to secure large bandages, slings, and any cloth item that needs to be held together.

☐ **Ear-loop masks (N-95).** Purchase a few children's size masks to use in case of chemical or smoke inhalation situations. I suggest even using them on days when the air quality is especially poor.

☐ **Hand sanitizer.** Put some in the first-aid kit, and scatter bottles around the house for easy access.

☐ **Lip balm.** When kids get sick, their lips can become very dry and may crack. Note also that chapped lips can be a sign of dehydration.

☐ **Nail clippers.** These come in small and very-small sizes for little hands and feet and baby's fingers and toes.

☐ **Nasal saline drops.** Use them to help alleviate nasal congestion when children are suffering from a cold, flu, or allergies.

☐ **Thermometers.** Glass mercury thermometers are no longer recommended because they can break and release their toxic contents into the environment, so pick up a couple of digital thermometers. Depending on the ages of your children or grandchildren, you may need to take a rectal temperature in which case you should label that thermometer accordingly and separate it from your oral thermometer. Another option is the temporal artery thermometer, which you sweep across your child's forehead to measure the temperature of the temporal artery in the forehead.

HOME REMEDIES AND SIMPLE SOLUTIONS

Not every health remedy has to be purchased off the shelves of your local drugstore. I bet if you open your pantry, you'll find some basic everyday products that may be useful in administering first aid or may offer a health benefit whether you're in the midst of an emergency or not. I call these home remedies because they're simple products that you likely already have at home and aren't formulated by a pharmaceutical company specifically to treat an injury or illness. You may be surprised to discover that vinegar has many virtues above and beyond its culinary specialties. I'd like to share those virtues as well as introduce you to some other home products that offer benefits beyond the obvious. I encourage you to give them a try. I'm sure you'll be pleased with the results.

APPLE CIDER VINEGAR (ACV)

You probably have vinegar in your pantry, and perhaps a few different kinds—cider, red wine, white, and balsamic—that you use in salad dressings and cooking. I used to keep a number of different kinds of vinegar for different uses, but now I store primarily apple cider vinegar for its health benefits and its many applications around the house. I purchase white vinegar for household chores, but for health benefits, I buy only those products that contain the "mother" of the vinegar since it includes probiotics and other beneficial bacteria. Here are the many ways I use ACV. Consider giving them a try to see if they work for you.

FOR YOUR HEALTH

Use as a healthy flavoring in foods to replace salt, which has been linked to high blood pressure.

Sipping a mixture of apple cider vinegar and water (1 to 2 tablespoons [15-30 ml] of vinegar to 8 ounces [237 ml] or more of water) may help in the following ways:

- ☐ block digestion of starch, which helps control blood sugar after eating
- ☐ clear up diarrhea
- ☐ ease diaphragm spasms that can cause hiccups
- ☐ drain sinuses and clear a stuffy nose
- ☐ relieve heartburn and indigestion

Apple cider vinegar can help reduce skin inflammation and itching by killing the irritating bacteria. Mix one part of vinegar to four parts of cool water. Soak a washcloth in the solution and apply it to the inflamed area for 5 to 10 minutes twice a day.

- ☐ To treat a yeast infection, bathe for three to five days in water mixed with 1 ½ cups (356 ml) of apple cider vinegar.
- ☐ I use apple cider vinegar on my hands and feet to relieve swollen joints. You may need to dilute it with water if you have sensitive skin.
- ☐ ACV can be a great treatment for a nail or foot fungus. Apply it directly to the infected area or soak your foot in a mixture of two parts water to one part vinegar. If you are diabetic consult your physician before using this formula.

- To ease a mild sunburn, soak a cloth in a solution that's one part vinegar to eight parts water and apply to your skin.

- Apple cider vinegar can add body and shine to your hair by removing buildup from shampoos and conditioners. Mix 2 tablespoons (30 ml) in a cup (237 ml) of water and pour through your hair. To help control dandruff, combine equal parts of ACV and water and massage into your scalp before you shampoo.

- Try gargling with ½ teaspoon of apple cider vinegar in a cup (237 ml) of water to kill bacteria around your gums, eliminate bad breath, and whiten teeth.

FOR A HEALTHY HOME

- To clean a tile or linoleum floor, add a cup (237 ml) of apple cider vinegar to a bucket of water and mop your floor.

- Mix 2 cups (473 ml) of vinegar with 1 cup (237 ml) of water in a spray bottle and use it to clean windows, countertops, sinks, toilets, shower walls, and tubs.

- Add ⅛ cup (30 ml) to your toilet to deodorize it.

- Mix equal parts of vinegar and water to clean mildew inside a refrigerator.

- Vinegar can also be used to kill unwanted weeds in your yard.

COCONUT OIL

I can't believe I spent most of my years as a mother without knowing about the benefits of coconut oil. Lately, I've learned of so many ways to use it other than for cooking and baking, so I decided to try it out, and I've been pleased with the results. Here's what I've discovered:

- You can use it as a skin lotion. I'm amazed at how it melts into your skin once warmed by your body heat. A little goes a long way. Try it on dry elbows and knees and chapped lips.

- Forgot to buy your makeup remover? My granddaughter forgot to bring hers once when she visited and was pleased with how well coconut oil worked.

- If you've run out of your usual diaper rash cream, try coconut oil.

- I have family members who seem to get cold sores frequently and have found coconut oil to be a lifesaver in clearing up these tender spots.

- Coconut oil generates a unique flavor when used to fry foods and works very well with recipes that require high temperature cooking.

RUBBING ALCOHOL

Rubbing alcohol should be your go-to antiseptic for sterilizing tweezers, needles, thermometers, any device you are going to use for a medicinal purpose. Here are a few other ways it can come in handy:

- Try dabbing a little on mosquito bites and cold sores to prompt healing.

- Rub on your feet to fight athlete's foot.

- If you have a fungus under your fingernail or toenail, try soaking your hand or foot in a 50/50 solution of water and rubbing alcohol to clear up the fungus.

- Put a little bit of rubbing alcohol on a small piece of cloth and use it to clean your computer keyboard, mouse, remotes, phones, and other items you handle every day.

EPSOM SALT

Growing up in a family with a single mother on a tight budget, we rarely went to the doctor. My mom relied on just a few remedies that we had at home and the one product we used all the time was Epsom salt, technically known as magnesium sulfate. Consider giving this old-fashioned remedy a try in your home.

☐ To relieve constipation, dissolve Epsom salt in 8 ounces (237 ml) of water and sip. You might want to add a little lemon juice to make it more palatable. Adults and children 12 years and older can take 2 up to 6 teaspoons (60 g) a day in water either as a single dose or two doses separated by 4 hours. Children between the ages of 2 and 11, should take no more then 1 or 2 teaspoons (10-20 g) of Epsom salt a day; again, dissolve in water taken once or divide into two servings.

☐ Lots of people swear by Epsom salt soaks to relieve sore feet and aching muscles and joints. Dissolve 2 cups (600 g) of salt in a gallon of warm water and sink your feet into the soothing solution or add 2 cups (600 g) of Epsom salt as you run your bathwater for a whole-body soak.

☐ An Epsom salt solution may ease removal of a splinter. Soak a towel in the Epsom solution and apply it to the area with the splinter for several minutes, or if you can, immerse the splintered area in the solution. Then use clean tweezers to take the splinter out.

☐ To soothe sunburn, mix Epsom salt with water to a toothpaste-like consistency and apply gently to the burned skin.

☐ Epsom salt may help your garden grow, particularly if your soil lacks magnesium. Mix 1 tablespoon (20 g) of Epsom salt in a gallon of water to spray on plants in your backyard garden as well as houseplants.

☐ Try sprinkling Epsom salt around the base of your plants to deter slugs. It will also give a little magnesium boost to your vegetables or flowers.

HYDROGEN PEROXIDE

The first time I heard about peroxide was in high school when the girls were talking about using it to bleach their hair. Who knew it could be used to bleach clothes, clean countertops, cure canker sores, ease toothaches, and so much more? It's another versatile product to add to your store of aids to help maintain your health and the health of your home.

Hydrogen peroxide sold for consumer use comes in a 3 percent concentration, which is safe for the uses I'll describe below. It's best not to swallow it though, and it can irritate tissue with prolonged use on a wound or sore. Let's take a look at all the wonders that peroxide can perform.

FOR YOUR HEALTH

☐ To treat canker sores or minor mouth abrasions or soreness caused by braces, dentures, or injuries to your mouth, pour a capful of hydrogen peroxide in your mouth, swish it around for at least a minute and spit it out. Limit this peroxide swish to no more than four times a day and no more than seven days in a row.

- To prevent an infection from developing in minor cuts, scrapes, and burns, an antibiotic ointment is sufficient, but if you run out, pour a small amount of hydrogen peroxide on the wounded area. Let it dry before applying a bandage.

- If you are suffering with a bad toothache and can't get to the dentist, try swishing a capful of peroxide around your mouth for a minute or two; then spit it out.

- To treat boils, fungus, and other skin infections, add half a bottle of peroxide to your bathwater. If your feet are plagued by any of these skin issues mix a 50/50 peroxide/water solution and soak your feet.

FOR YOUR HEALTHY HOME

- To help kill germs in your kitchen and bathroom spray some hydrogen peroxide on a cloth and wipe down countertops and other surfaces that your hands or food come in contact with, including cutting boards and the handles on your refrigerator, stove, and kitchen and bathroom drawers.

- You can clean windows and mirrors with hydrogen peroxide, which won't streak like some cleaners do.

- If you've run out of bleach for laundering your whites, substitute hydrogen peroxide—a cup (237 ml) per load should make your clothes bright.

GET CERT-IFIED

While first-aid training is important and essential for anyone who wants to be prepared to handle a medical emergency, you might consider going a step further and enrolling in C.E.R.T. training. This program will teach you basic disaster response skills for assisting others in your neighborhood, workplace, or wherever you find yourself if a disaster strikes and professional responders are unable to get to you right away. My husband and I went through C.E.R.T. training. It is very hands-on. We wrapped bandages on live people, attached splints to their legs, enacted the procedures to follow if someone is going into shock, applied a temporary tourniquet, and practiced many other first-aid procedures.

One of the most difficult training sessions was when we were divided into small teams and sent into a darkened room where people from the local school pretended to be suffering from the effects of an earthquake. We used flashlights to search for people among the fallen debris that had been staged, and we were taught how to use triage—the process of evaluating the seriousness of injuries to individuals on a scale so they can be treated according to the severity of their injuries. It was an eye-opening lesson, but I'm glad we went through this program and that we are now better prepared to assist in any emergency.

If you think you might be interested in C.E.R.T. training, visit fema.gov/community-emergency-response-teams where you can learn more and find a list of programs near you.

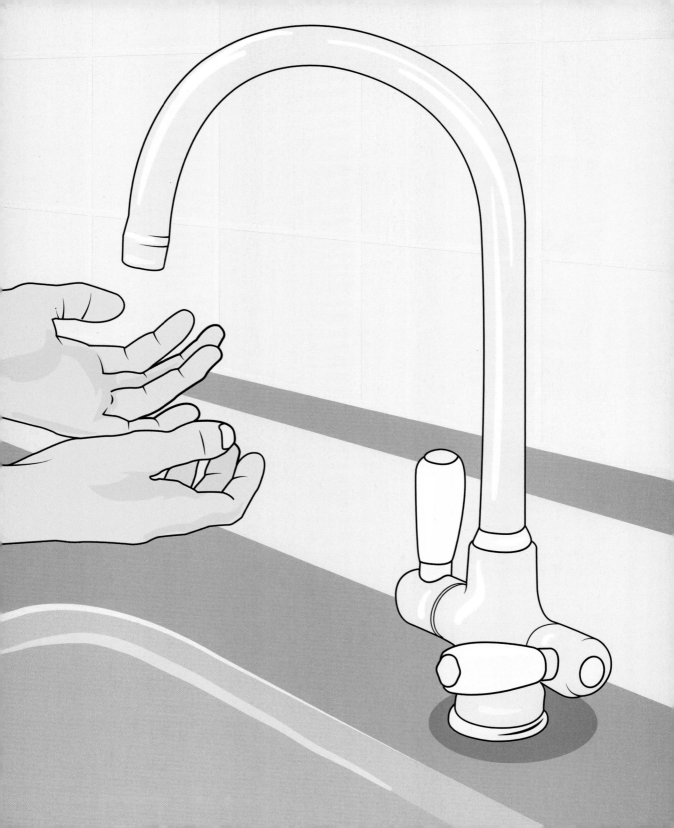

CHAPTER 6
HYGIENE FOR YOU AND YOUR HOME

You flip the handle on the faucet—nothing. You learn that there's been a serious break in the water lines, and it will take days, maybe a week, for water to be restored to your home. How will you wash your hands, your face, bathe, brush your teeth?

In this chapter, you'll learn how to keep yourself and your family clean and safe when running water is gone. I'll teach you how to assemble two versions of an emergency toilet, and how to make your own family cloths in the event you run out of toilet paper. You'll also learn just what to store for your family so that you have enough hygiene items to stay clean in an emergency or disaster situation.

There's nothing more refreshing or soothing than taking a shower or bath—washing your hair and scrubbing your body. It cleanses all the sweat and grime from a day working in the heat, and it warms you up on cold winter mornings or after you've come off the ski slopes. Here in the United States, most of us get to enjoy a shower or bath several times a week if not daily. And consider how many times you wash your hands every day under clean running water from your bathroom faucet. But it can all change in an instant.

It's one thing to lose electricity. You won't have freely flowing hot water (unless you have a gas water heater), but you'll have water, and the adventurous among us can take cold showers or sponge baths, or there's the option of heating up water with one of your emergency cooking devices. But if the water supply to your home is cut off, then all the H_2O you'll have will be what you've stored plus what you can purify from a nearby lake or stream or a rain barrel or backyard pool if you have them.

Perhaps post-hurricane or post-earthquake, water is still flowing into your home but has become contaminated. I read about a small town in southern Idaho where the capacity of the water treatment plant was exceeded due to the volume of snowmelt and heavy rains. All residents were asked to boil their water before drinking or cooking with it because sediment coming into the treatment plant carried parasites and bacteria at levels that the chlorine could not eliminate. You don't want to drink contaminated water. You don't want to cook with it. And you don't want to wash your dishes with it or bathe in it. You need to be able to purify contaminated water by boiling it, filtering it, or adding a small amount of bleach or other water treatment product (see Chapter 1 for a complete discussion of water purification and storage). When clean water is at a premium, as it is in many emergency situations, you'll need to create a new routine for bathing, shampooing your hair, and washing your dishes. Let's begin with personal hygiene.

FLOODWATER WARNING

The Centers for Disease Control and Prevention warns that you should not use floodwater under any circumstances. Boiling it or any other attempt at purifying the floodwater may not sufficiently eliminate harmful bacteria and parasites. And if you come in contact with floodwater, be sure to clean your hands with hand sanitizer or wet wipes before eating any food.

BATHING AND BRUSHING YOUR TEETH

Washing up is not only important for your physical health but for your mental well-being. The first couple of days after a disaster, you probably won't mind going without a shower, but with the fourth or fifth day as body grime and odor builds, you begin to feel just plain yucky. It's one thing to spend a week camping where everyone smells like the fire pit. It's another thing if you're at home and accustomed to showering and shampooing, flossing and brushing your teeth every morning. Several consecutive days of feeling unclean and unkempt can get depressing. When you're struggling with the challenges of the aftermath of a disaster, a little cleanliness can go a long way in refreshing your body and your spirit.

Again, if you have water coming into the home that's clean but cold or that's contaminated but can be purified by boiling, filtering, or other means, you'll have plenty for brushing your teeth and washing your hands and face, and you'll be able to take sponge baths and shampoo your hair. You may not have the convenience of the daily shower, but you'll be able to wash up with water and enjoy the pleasure of feeling refreshed.

If you're limited to the water you've stored, you're personal hygiene plan changes. The amount of water I recommended for storage in Chapter 1—four gallons (15 L) per person per day—covers drinking, cooking, washing dishes, laundering your underwear, and the bare minimum of personal hygiene. You'll have enough to brush your teeth daily and shampoo your hair once a week. Depending on how much you've been able to store before disaster strikes and how long you'll be without water, you'll want to be very conservative with that water.

YOUR EMERGENCY PERSONAL HYGIENE PLAN

When clean water has stopped flowing into your home, follow these guidelines for washing up, using the least amount of water.

- ☐ When brushing your teeth, use only the water necessary to rinse your mouth.
- ☐ To wash your face, use just enough water to wet your washcloth.
- ☐ Shampoo your hair just once a week.
- ☐ Use wet wipes for a sponge bath.
- ☐ Use hand sanitizer or wet wipes to wash your hands.

WHAT YOU NEED TO STORE

As you build your storage of water and food, you'll also want to stash some extra items for personal hygiene. Include hand moisturizer and body lotion because hand sanitizer and wet wipes tend to dry out your skin. I like to have a bar of soap around to use when bathing a baby or to scrub out stains on clothes. I can also use it with water from a lake or swimming pool. Plus if we need to go to a temporary emergency facility such as a church or high school, which have showers, I will have my own bar of soap. Finally, I recommend that you store extra toothbrushes above and beyond what your family needs in case you have guests during an emergency. Here are my storage recommendations:

FOR A COUPLE

For 3 days

- ☐ 2 toothbrushes (plus extras for guests)
- ☐ 1 (6-oz [170-g]) tube of toothpaste
- ☐ 1 container of dental floss
- ☐ 1 (8-oz [237-ml]) bottle of shampoo
- ☐ 1 box of wet wipes (100 per container)
- ☐ 1 (8-oz [237-ml]) bottle of hand sanitizer
- ☐ 1 bar of soap
- ☐ 1 (8-oz [237-ml]) tube or bottle of hand moisturizer
- ☐ 1 (8-oz [237-ml]) bottle of body lotion

For 7 days

- ☐ 2 toothbrushes (plus extras for guests)
- ☐ 1 (6-oz [170-g]) tube of toothpaste
- ☐ 1 container of dental floss
- ☐ 1 (8-oz [237-ml]) bottle of shampoo
- ☐ 1 box of wet wipes (100 per container)
- ☐ 2 (8-oz [237-ml]) bottles of hand sanitizer
- ☐ 1 bar of soap
- ☐ 1 (8-oz [237-ml]) tube or bottle of hand moisturizer
- ☐ 1 (8-oz [237-ml]) bottle of body lotion

For 1 month

- ☐ 2 toothbrushes (plus extras for guests)
- ☐ 1 (6-oz [170-g]) tube of toothpaste
- ☐ 1 container of dental floss
- ☐ 1 (8-oz [237-ml]) bottle of shampoo
- ☐ 2 boxes of wet wipes (100 per container)
- ☐ 4 (8-oz [237-ml]) bottles of hand sanitizer
- ☐ 1 bar of soap
- ☐ 1 (8-oz [237-ml]) tube or bottle of hand moisturizer
- ☐ 1 (8-oz [237-ml]) bottle of body lotion

FOR A FAMILY OF THREE

For 3 days

- ☐ 3 toothbrushes (plus extras for guests)
- ☐ 1 (6-oz [170-g]) tube of toothpaste
- ☐ 1 container of dental floss
- ☐ 1 (8-oz [237-ml]) bottle of shampoo
- ☐ 1 box of wet wipes (100 per container)
- ☐ 1 (8-oz [237-ml]) bottle of hand sanitizer
- ☐ 1 bar of soap
- ☐ 1 (8-oz [237-ml]) tube or bottle of hand moisturizer
- ☐ 1 (8-oz [237-ml]) bottle of body lotion

For 7 days

- ☐ 3 toothbrushes (plus extras for guests)
- ☐ 1 (6-oz [170-g]) tube of toothpaste
- ☐ 1 container of dental floss
- ☐ 1 (8-oz [237-ml]) bottle of shampoo
- ☐ 2 boxes of wet wipes (100 per container)
- ☐ 2 (8-oz [237-ml]) bottles of hand sanitizer
- ☐ 1 bar of soap
- ☐ 1 (8-oz [237-ml]) tube or bottle of hand moisturizer
- ☐ 1 (8-oz [237-ml]) bottle of body lotion

For 1 month

- ☐ 3 toothbrushes (plus extras for guests)
- ☐ 2 (6-oz [170-g]) tubes of toothpaste
- ☐ 2 containers of dental floss
- ☐ 1 (8-oz [237-ml]) bottle of shampoo
- ☐ 8 boxes of wet wipes (100 per container)
- ☐ 8 (8-oz [237-ml]) bottles of hand sanitizer
- ☐ 2 bars of soap
- ☐ 2 (8-oz [237-ml]) tubes or bottles of hand moisturizer
- ☐ 2 (8-oz [237-ml]) bottles of body lotion

FOR A FAMILY OF FOUR

For 3 days

- ☐ 4 toothbrushes (plus extras for guests)
- ☐ 1 (6-oz [170-g]) tube of toothpaste
- ☐ 1 container of dental floss
- ☐ 1 (8-oz [237-ml]) bottle of shampoo
- ☐ 2 boxes of wet wipes (100 per container)
- ☐ 2 (8-oz [237-ml]) bottles of hand sanitizer
- ☐ 1 bar of soap

- ☐ 1 (8-oz [237-ml]) tube or bottle of hand moisturizer
- ☐ 1 (8-oz [237-ml]) bottle of body lotion

For 7 days

- ☐ 4 toothbrushes (plus extras for guests)
- ☐ 1 (6-oz [170-g]) tube of toothpaste
- ☐ 1 container of dental floss
- ☐ 1 (8-oz [237-ml]) bottle of shampoo
- ☐ 2 boxes of wet wipes (100 per container)
- ☐ 2 (8-oz [237-ml]) bottles of hand sanitizer
- ☐ 1 bar of soap
- ☐ 2 (8-oz [237-ml]) tubes or bottles of hand moisturizer
- ☐ 2 (8-oz [237-ml]) bottles of body lotion

For 1 month

- ☐ 4 toothbrushes (plus extras for guests)
- ☐ 2 (6-oz [170-g]) tubes of toothpaste
- ☐ 2 containers of dental floss
- ☐ 2 (8-oz [237-ml]) bottles of shampoo
- ☐ 3 boxes of wet wipes (100 per container)
- ☐ 8 (8-oz [237-ml]) bottles of hand sanitizer
- ☐ 1 bar of soap
- ☐ 2 (8-oz [237-ml]) tubes or bottles of hand moisturizer
- ☐ 2 (8-oz [237-ml]) bottles of body lotion

FOR A FAMILY OF FIVE

For 3 days

- ☐ 5 toothbrushes (plus extras for guests)
- ☐ 1 (6-oz [170-g]) tube of toothpaste
- ☐ 1 container of dental floss

(continued)

- ☐ 1 (8-oz [237-ml]) bottle of shampoo
- ☐ 1 box of wet wipes (100 per container)
- ☐ 2 (8-oz [237-ml]) bottles of hand sanitizer
- ☐ 1 bar of soap
- ☐ 2 (8-oz [237-ml]) tubes or bottles of hand moisturizer
- ☐ 2 (8-oz [237-ml]) bottles of body lotion

For 7 days
- ☐ 5 toothbrushes (plus extras for guests)
- ☐ 1 (6-oz [170-g]) tube of toothpaste
- ☐ 1 container of dental floss
- ☐ 1 (8-oz [237-ml]) bottle of shampoo
- ☐ 3 boxes of wet wipes (100 per container)
- ☐ 3 (8-oz [237-ml]) bottles of hand sanitizer
- ☐ 1 bar of soap
- ☐ 3 (8-oz [237-ml]) tubes or bottles of hand moisturizer
- ☐ 3 (8-oz [237-ml]) bottles of body lotion

For 1 month
- ☐ 5 toothbrushes (plus extras for guests)
- ☐ 2 (6-oz [170-g]) tubes of toothpaste
- ☐ 2 containers of dental floss
- ☐ 2 (8-oz [237-ml]) bottles of shampoo
- ☐ 4 boxes of wet wipes (100 per container)
- ☐ 10 (8-oz [237-ml]) bottles of hand sanitizer
- ☐ 2 bars of soap
- ☐ 3 (8-oz [237-ml]) tubes or bottles of hand moisturizer
- ☐ 3 (8-oz [237-ml]) bottles of body lotion

Note: You might see an expiration date on wet wipes because they will dry out if kept too long in storage, so try to rotate them so they stay fresh. If they do dry out, you can use them with water to wash dishes.

USING THE TOILET

Indoor plumbing is yet another amenity we take for granted. The days of heading outside to use the outhouse are long past. But if the water or sewer lines are broken or shut down, you might wish you had an outhouse because you won't be able to flush your toilet unless you first pour water into the toilet bowl, and flushing uses a lot of water—1.6 gallons (6 L) if you have a standard toilet and 3.5 to 7 gallons (13-26 L) for an older model.

Think about how many times your family flushes the toilet each day. Give it your best guess, or if you want to be more precise, post a sticky note and pencil in your bathroom, and for one 24-hour period, ask everyone in your family to record a hash mark on that sticky note after each flush. Multiply that number by 1.6 gallons (6 L) to determine the least amount of water your toilet uses in a day. Pick a day when you're all home because that will most closely resemble your situation in a disaster.

Let's do a hypothetical estimate for a family of four, assuming the following number of bathroom trips: first thing in the morning, midmorning, lunchtime, afternoon, dinnertime, evening, before bed—6 times minimum. Six flushes per person for four people equals 24 flushes. At 1.6 gallons (6 L) per flush, that's 38.4 gallons (145 L) a day down the sewer lines—more than two days of clean water storage for a family of four. Now if you lived on a lake and could haul water to your bathroom to flush the toilet, great, you're set, but most of us will have only the water we've stored, so we need a toilet alternative.

BATHROOM WATER USE

The United States Environmental Protection Agency offers these estimates for water flow in a typical bathroom:

Toilet, standard: 1.6 gallons (6 L) per flush

Toilet, older models: 3.5 to 7 gallons (13-26 L) per flush

Showerhead: 2.5 gallons (9 L) per minute

Faucet: 2 gallons (8 L) per minute
Source: epa.gov/WaterSense/pubs/indoor.html

EMERGENCY TOILETS

When flushing is not an option, I have two simple plans for creating an in-house emergency toilet. For the first you will need the following items:

☐ A box of heavy-duty, 33-gallon (125-L) black garbage bags

☐ A box of 10- or 13-gallon (38-L–49-L) garbage bags

☐ A roll of duct tape (9 mm–2 in [5 cm] by 60 yd [55 M])

☐ A bag/container of kitty litter

☐ A 1-cup (237-ml) measure

☐ A kitty-litter scooper

☐ Toilet paper

You may not have thought about not being able to flush your toilet in an emergency. A few garbage bags and kitty litter can solve the problem.

HERE'S WHAT YOU DO

1. Turn off the water to the toilet.

2. Tape the handle so that no one can flush the toilet accidentally.

3. Lift the toilet lid and place one 33-gallon (125-L) garbage bag in the toilet, draping it over the bowl.

4. If you have kids, I would tape the bag onto the tank to keep the bag in place.

5. Put 2 cups (283 g) of kitty litter in the bag.

As the toilet is used, scoop the waste into one of the smaller garbage bags, which you can secure with a knot and place outside your house in a 33-gallon (125-L) black bag for pickup or disposal.

STORE THIS ADVICE

You can buy a box of 500 (10-gallon [38-L]) garbage bags online at a low cost but 13-gallon (49-L) bags are more common in local supermarkets.

WHAT YOU NEED TO STORE

To prepare for an emergency, here's what you need to store to build and use this toilet.

FOR A COUPLE

For 3 days

- ☐ 3 (33-gallon [125-L]) heavy-duty black garbage bags
- ☐ 1 roll of duct tape (9 mm–2 in [5 cm] by 60 yd [55 M])
- ☐ 1 (8–10-lb [3.6–4.5-kg]) bag of kitty litter
- ☐ 1 kitty-litter scooper
- ☐ 1 (1-cup [237-ml]) measure
- ☐ 3 (10- or 13-gallon [38–49-L]) garbage bags for disposal
- ☐ 2 rolls of toilet paper

For 1 week

- ☐ 7 (33-gallon [125-L]) heavy-duty black garbage bags
- ☐ 1 roll of duct tape (9 mm–2 in [5 cm] by 60 yd [55 M])
- ☐ 1 (8–10-lb [3.6–4.5-kg]) bag of kitty litter
- ☐ 1 kitty-litter scooper
- ☐ 1 (1-cup [237-ml]) measure
- ☐ 7 (10- or 13-gallon [38–49-L]) garbage bags for disposal
- ☐ 2 rolls of toilet paper

For 1 month

- ☐ 30 (33-gallon [125-L]) heavy-duty black garbage bags
- ☐ 1 roll of duct tape (9 mm–2 in [5 cm] by 60 yd [55 M])
- ☐ 1 (30-lb [13.6-kg]) bag of kitty litter
- ☐ 1 kitty-litter scooper
- ☐ 1 (1-cup [237-ml]) measure
- ☐ 30 (10- or 13-gallon [38–49-L]) garbage bags for disposal
- ☐ 16 rolls of toilet paper

FOR A FAMILY OF THREE

For 3 days

- ☐ 3 (33-gallon [125-L]) heavy-duty black garbage bags
- ☐ 1 roll of duct tape (9 mm–2 in [5 cm] by 60 yd [55 M])
- ☐ 1 (8–10-lb [3.6–4.5-kg]) bag of kitty litter
- ☐ 1 kitty-litter scooper
- ☐ 1 (1-cup [237-ml]) measure
- ☐ 3 (10- or 13-gallon [38–49-L]) garbage bags for disposal
- ☐ 2 rolls of toilet paper

For 1 week

- ☐ 7 (33-gallon [125-L]) heavy-duty black garbage bags
- ☐ 1 roll of duct tape (9 mm–2 in [5 cm] by 60 yd [55 M])
- ☐ 1 (8–10-lb [3.6–4.5-kg]) bag of kitty litter
- ☐ 1 kitty-litter scooper
- ☐ 1 (1-cup [237-ml]) measure
- ☐ 7 (10- or 13-gallon [38–49-L]) garbage bags for disposal
- ☐ 4 rolls of toilet paper

For 1 month

- ☐ 30 (33-gallon [125-L]) heavy-duty black garbage bags
- ☐ 1 roll of duct tape (9 mm–2 in [5 cm] by 60 yd [55 M])
- ☐ 1 (30-lb [13.6-kg]) bag of kitty litter
- ☐ 1 kitty-litter scooper
- ☐ 1 (1-cup [237-ml]) measure
- ☐ 30 (10- or 13-gallon [38–49-L]) garbage bags for disposal
- ☐ 16 rolls of toilet paper

(continued)

FOR A FAMILY OF FOUR

For 3 days

- ☐ 3 (33-gallon [125-L]) heavy-duty black garbage bags
- ☐ 1 roll of duct tape (9 mm–2 in [5 cm] by 60 yd [55 M])
- ☐ 1 (16–20-lb [7.2–9-kg]) bag of kitty litter
- ☐ 1 kitty-litter scooper
- ☐ 1 (1-cup [237-ml]) measure
- ☐ 3 (10- or 13-gallon [38–49-L]) garbage bags for disposal
- ☐ 4 rolls of toilet paper

For 1 week

- ☐ 7 (33-gallon [125-L]) heavy-duty black garbage bags
- ☐ 1 roll of duct tape (9 mm–2 in [5 cm] by 60 yd [55 M])
- ☐ 1 (16–20-lb [7.2–9-kg]) bag of kitty litter
- ☐ 1 kitty-litter scooper
- ☐ 1 (1-cup [237-ml]) measure
- ☐ 7 (10- or 13-gallon [38–49-L]) garbage bags for disposal
- ☐ 8 rolls of toilet paper

For 1 month

- ☐ 30 (33-gallon [125-L]) heavy-duty black garbage bags
- ☐ 1 roll of duct tape (9 mm–2 in [5 cm] by 60 yd [55 M])
- ☐ 1 (60-lb [27.2-kg]) bag of kitty litter
- ☐ 1 kitty-litter scooper
- ☐ 1 (1-cup [237-ml]) measure
- ☐ 30 (10- or 13-gallon [38–49-L]) garbage bags for disposal
- ☐ 32 rolls of toilet paper

FOR A FAMILY OF FIVE

For 3 days

- ☐ 3 (33-gallon [125-L]) heavy-duty black garbage bags
- ☐ 1 roll of duct tape (9 mm–2 in [5 cm] by 60 yd [55 M])
- ☐ 1 (16–20-lb [7.2–9-kg]) bag of kitty litter
- ☐ 1 kitty-litter scooper
- ☐ 1 (1-cup [237-ml]) measure
- ☐ 3 (10- or 13-gallon [38–49-L]) garbage bags for disposal
- ☐ 4 rolls of toilet paper

For 1 week

- ☐ 7 (33-gallon [125-L]) heavy-duty black garbage bags
- ☐ 1 roll of duct tape (9 mm–2 in [5 cm] by 60 yd [55 M])
- ☐ 1 (16–20-lb [7.2–9-kg]) bag of kitty litter
- ☐ 1 kitty-litter scooper
- ☐ 1 (1-cup [237-ml]) measure
- ☐ 7 (10- or 13-gallon [38–49-L]) garbage bags for disposal
- ☐ 8 rolls of toilet paper

For 1 month

- ☐ 30 (33-gallon [125-L]) heavy-duty black garbage bags
- ☐ 1 roll of duct tape (9 mm–2 in [5 cm] by 60 yd [55 M])
- ☐ 1 (60-lb [27.2-kg]) bag of kitty litter
- ☐ 1 kitty-litter scooper
- ☐ 1 (1-cup [237-ml]) measure
- ☐ 30 (10- or 13-gallon [38–49-L]) garbage bags for disposal
- ☐ 32 rolls of toilet paper

I always like to have two ways of solving a problem. For my second emergency toilet option, you'll need the following supplies:

- ☐ 6-gallon (23-L) bucket (I prefer 6-gallon [23-L] over 5-gallon [19-L] buckets because you don't have to squat down as far. You can order 6-gallon [23-L] buckets online from Amazon.com or EmergencyEssentials.com)
- ☐ 10- or 13-gallon (38–49-L) garbage bags to line the bucket
- ☐ Duct tape (9 mm–2 in [5 cm] by 60 yd [55 M])
- ☐ An emergency toilet seat with lid (I like the Tote-able Toilet Seat and Lid from Emergency Essentials because it has a lip that fits on the 6-gallon buckets)
- ☐ Kitty-litter (I buy 8–10-lb [3.6–4.5-kg]) bags to fit inside the bucket)
- ☐ Kitty-litter scooper
- ☐ 33-gallon (125-L) heavy-duty black garbage bags for disposal
- ☐ Toilet paper

You can store all of the supplies inside the bucket until you need to use it. When the need arises, place one bag inside the bucket with the excess folded over the outside of the bucket and secure it with duct tape. Add 2 cups (283 g) of kitty litter to the bag and place the toilet lid on top of the bucket. As you use the emergency toilet, scoop out the waste matter into a bag for disposal.

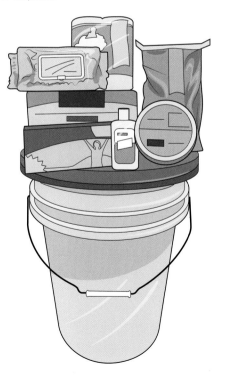

In an emergency you may have to evacuate from your home. If so, and a shelter isn't available, you'll need one of these portable units to satisfy your need to "go."

WHAT YOU NEED TO STORE

To prepare for an emergency, here's what you need to store to make this toilet:

FOR A COUPLE

For 3 days

- ☐ 1 (6-gallon [23-L]) bucket
- ☐ 3 (10- or 13-gallon [38–49-L]) garbage bags to line the bucket
- ☐ 1 roll duct tape (9 mm–2 in [5 cm] by 60 yd [55 M])
- ☐ 1 emergency toilet seat with lid
- ☐ 1 (8–10-lb [3.6–4.5-kg]) bag of kitty litter
- ☐ 1 (1-cup [237-ml]) measure
- ☐ 1 kitty-litter scooper
- ☐ 3 (33-gallon [125-L]) heavy-duty black garbage bags for disposal
- ☐ 2 rolls of toilet paper

For 1 week

- ☐ 1 (6-gallon [23-L]) bucket
- ☐ 7 (10- or 13-gallon [38–49-L]) garbage bags to line the bucket
- ☐ 1 roll duct tape (9 mm–2 in [5 cm] by 60 yd [55 M])
- ☐ 1 emergency toilet seat with lid
- ☐ 1 (8–10-lb [3.6–4.5-kg] bag of kitty litter
- ☐ 1 (1-cup [237-ml]) measure
- ☐ 1 kitty-litter scooper
- ☐ 7 (33-gallon [125-L]) heavy-duty black garbage bags for disposal
- ☐ 4 rolls of toilet paper

For 1 month

- ☐ 1 (6-gallon [23-L]) bucket
- ☐ 30 (10- or 13-gallon [38–49-L]) garbage bags to line the bucket
- ☐ 1 roll duct tape (9 mm–2 in [5 cm] by 60 yd [55 M])

- ☐ 1 emergency toilet seat with lid
- ☐ 1 (30-lb [13.6-kg]) bag of kitty litter
- ☐ 1 (1-cup [237-ml]) measure
- ☐ 1 kitty-litter scooper
- ☐ 30 (33-gallon [125-L]) heavy-duty black garbage bags for disposal
- ☐ 16 rolls of toilet paper

FOR A FAMILY OF THREE

For 3 days

- ☐ 1 (6-gallon [23-L]) bucket
- ☐ 3 (10- or 13-gallon [38–49-L]) garbage bags to line the bucket
- ☐ 1 roll duct tape (9 mm–2 in [5 cm] by 60 yd [55 M])
- ☐ 1 emergency toilet seat with lid
- ☐ 1 (8-10 lb [3.6–4.5-kg]) bag of kitty litter
- ☐ 1 (1-cup [237-ml]) measure
- ☐ 1 kitty-litter scooper
- ☐ 3 (33-gallon [125-L]) heavy-duty black garbage bags for disposal
- ☐ 2 rolls of toilet paper

For 1 week

- ☐ 1 (6-gallon [23-L]) bucket
- ☐ 7 (10- or 13-gallon [38–49-L]) garbage bags to line the bucket
- ☐ 1 roll duct tape (9 mm–2 in [5 cm] by 60 yd [55 M])
- ☐ 1 emergency toilet seat with lid
- ☐ 1 (8-10 lb [3.6–4.5-kg]) bag of kitty litter
- ☐ 1 (1-cup [237-ml]) measure
- ☐ 1 kitty-litter scooper

- [ ] 7 (33-gallon [125-L]) heavy-duty black garbage bags for disposal
- [ ] 4 rolls of toilet paper

For 1 month

- [ ] 1 (6-gallon [23-L]) bucket
- [ ] 30 (10- or 13-gallon [38–49-L]) garbage bags to line the bucket
- [ ] 1 roll duct tape (9 mm–2 in [5 cm] by 60 yd [55 M])
- [ ] 1 emergency toilet seat with lid
- [ ] 1 (30-lb [13.6-kg]) bag of kitty litter
- [ ] 1 (1-cup [237-ml]) measure
- [ ] 1 kitty-litter scooper
- [ ] 30 (33-gallon [125-L]) heavy-duty black garbage bags for disposal
- [ ] 16 rolls of toilet paper

FOR A FAMILY OF FOUR

For 3 days

- [ ] 1 (6-gallon [23-L]) bucket
- [ ] 3 (10- or 13-gallon [38–49-L]) garbage bags to line the bucket
- [ ] 1 roll duct tape (9 mm–2 in by 60 yd [55 M])
- [ ] 1 emergency toilet seat with lid
- [ ] 1 (16-20 lb [7.2-9-kg]) bag of kitty litter
- [ ] 1 (1-cup [237-ml]) measure
- [ ] 1 kitty-litter scooper
- [ ] 3 (33-gallon [125-L]) heavy-duty black garbage bags for disposal
- [ ] 4 rolls of toilet paper

For 1 week

- [ ] 1 (6-gallon [23-L]) bucket
- [ ] 7 (10- or 13-gallon [38–49-L]) garbage bags to line the bucket
- [ ] 1 roll duct tape (9 mm–2 in [5 cm] by 60 yd [55 M])

- [ ] 1 emergency toilet seat with lid
- [ ] 1 (16–20-lb [7.2-9-kg]) bag of kitty litter
- [ ] 1 (1-cup [237-ml]) measure
- [ ] 1 kitty-litter scooper
- [ ] 7 (33-gallon [125-L]) heavy-duty black garbage bags for disposal
- [ ] 8 rolls of toilet paper

For 1 month

- [ ] 1 (6-gallon [23-L]) bucket
- [ ] 30 (10- or 13-gallon [38–49-L]) garbage bags to line the bucket
- [ ] 1 roll duct tape (9 mm–2 in [5 cm] by 60 yd [55 M])
- [ ] 1 emergency toilet seat with lid
- [ ] 1 (60-lb [27.2-kg]) bag of kitty litter
- [ ] 1 (1-cup [237-ml]) measure
- [ ] 1 kitty-litter scooper
- [ ] 30 (33-gallon [125-L]) heavy-duty black garbage bags for disposal
- [ ] 32 rolls of toilet paper

FOR A FAMILY OF FIVE

For 3 days

- [ ] 1 (6-gallon [23-L]) bucket
- [ ] 3 (10- or 13-gallon [38–49-L]) garbage bags to line the bucket
- [ ] 1 roll duct tape (9 mm–2 in [5 cm] by 60 yd [55 M])
- [ ] 1 emergency toilet seat with lid
- [ ] 1 (16–20-lb [7.2-9-kg]) bag of kitty litter
- [ ] 1 (1-cup [237-ml]) measure
- [ ] 1 kitty-litter scooper
- [ ] 3 (33-gallon [125-L]) heavy-duty black garbage bags for disposal
- [ ] 4 rolls of toilet paper

(continued)

For 1 week

- ☐ 1 (6-gallon [23-L]) bucket
- ☐ 7 (10- or 13-gallon [38–49-L]) garbage bags to line the bucket
- ☐ 1 roll duct tape (9 mm–2 in [5 cm] by 60 yd [55 M])
- ☐ 1 emergency toilet seat with lid
- ☐ 1 (16-20 lb [7.2–9-kg]) bag of kitty litter
- ☐ 1 (1-cup [237-ml]) measure
- ☐ 1 kitty-litter scooper
- ☐ 7 (33-gallon [125-L]) heavy-duty black garbage bags for disposal
- ☐ 8 rolls of toilet paper

For 1 month

- ☐ 1 (6-gallon [23-L]) bucket
- ☐ 30 (10- or 13-gallon [38–49-L]) garbage bags to line the bucket
- ☐ 1 roll duct tape (9 mm–2 in [5 cm] by 60 yd [55 M])
- ☐ 1 emergency toilet seat with lid
- ☐ 1 (60-lb [27.2-kg]) bag of kitty litter
- ☐ 1 (1-cup [237-ml]) measure
- ☐ 1 kitty-litter scooper
- ☐ 30 (33-gallon [125-L]) heavy-duty black garbage bags for disposal
- ☐ 32 rolls of toilet paper

WASTE DISPOSAL

How do you dispose of bathroom waste when you can't flush it away? If garbage pickup services are delayed, hopefully your local authorities will set up disposal sites where you can take your bags. If not, you will want to bury it since human waste carries bacteria that can cause serious disease. You'll need to dig a hole at least 3 feet (1 M) deep located several hundred feet from any water source. You can also burn the bags away from your home in a hole to contain the fire.

FAMILY CLOTHS

I keep on hand three to six months of toilet paper in case of an emergency, but recently I decided to make family cloths to use if I ever run out of toilet paper. You could always use leaves—other than, of course, poison ivy and other itch-inducing plants—but that's not my thing. So I take some nice soft flannel in two different colors—one color for pee and the other for poop—and I cut out 9-inch (23-cm) squares. And I store them in separate wastebaskets. Use a squirt bottle to rinse, wipe with the flannel cloth, and toss in the wastebasket. You can wash these and reuse them. The family cloths should be washed separately from your other clothes because of possible E.coli and bacteria contamination.

Consider storing family cloths to use in case you run out of toilet paper in an emergency.

OTHER HYGIENE NEEDS

Don't forget to store an extra month's worth at least of feminine hygiene products for the young women in your household. Also, if you have a baby, know that disposable diapers are among the first things to disappear from the grocery store shelves after a disaster. Stock up on two-dozen prefolded cloth diapers as well as the waterproof pants and diaper pins to go with them.

CLEANING YOUR HOUSE

Keeping your home clean can be as important as washing your hands when it comes to preventing the spread of germs that might potentially make you ill. A clean home is a healthy home and a happy one. Just as washing the day's sweat and grime from your skin can keep your spirits up so can a clean kitchen and bathroom. When the water supply to your home gets cut off or becomes contaminated, however, you can forget using the dishwasher or mopping your floors with buckets full of water. If you've been able to store plenty of water before disaster struck, you'll have enough to clean your dishes, but use it sparingly. If you're worried about having enough water to last your emergency situation (remember the formula: 4 gallons [15 L] per person per day), use paper plates and cups and plastic utensils. I always keep these products in my storage stash, packing them in larger bags and storing them in a dry place in my home to protect them from moisture (see "Paper Dishes and Plastic Utensils" on the next page for recommended storage quantitites).

PAPER DISHES AND PLASTIC UTENSILS

It's best to be ready with paper plates, bowls, and cups, just in case the water is shut off and you need to conserve the water you have stored and not use it to wash dishes. Even if there is ample water available you may want a break from doing dishes some nights. Here's what you should plan to store, assuming three meals a day per person:

FOR A COUPLE

For 3 days

- ☐ 6 of each: paper plates, bowls, and cups
- ☐ 6 of each: plastic forks, knives, and spoons
- ☐ 6 paper napkins
- ☐ 1 roll of paper towels

For 7 days

- ☐ 14 of each: paper plates, bowls, and cups
- ☐ 14 of each: plastic forks, knives, and spoons
- ☐ 14 paper napkins
- ☐ 2 rolls of paper towels

For 1 month

- ☐ 60 of each: paper plates, bowls, and cups
- ☐ 60 of each: plastic forks, knives, and spoons
- ☐ 60 paper napkins
- ☐ 8 rolls of paper towels

FOR A FAMILY OF THREE

For 3 days

- ☐ 9 of each: paper plates, bowls, and cups
- ☐ 9 of each: plastic forks, knives, and spoons
- ☐ 9 paper napkins
- ☐ 1 roll of paper towels

For 7 days

- ☐ 21 of each: paper plates, bowls, and cups
- ☐ 21 of each: plastic forks, knives, and spoons
- ☐ 21 paper napkins
- ☐ 2 rolls of paper towels

For 1 month

- ☐ 90 of each: paper plates, bowls, and cups
- ☐ 90 of each: plastic forks, knives, and spoons
- ☐ 90 paper napkins
- ☐ 8 rolls of paper towels

FOR A FAMILY OF FOUR

For 3 days

- ☐ 12 of each: paper plates, bowls, and cups
- ☐ 12 of each: plastic forks, knives, and spoons
- ☐ 12 paper napkins
- ☐ 2 rolls of paper towels

For 7 days

- ☐ 28 of each: paper plates, bowls, and cups
- ☐ 28 of each: plastic forks, knives, and spoons
- ☐ 28 paper napkins
- ☐ 4 rolls of paper towels

For 1 month

- ☐ 120 of each: paper plates, bowls, and cups
- ☐ 120 of each: plastic forks, knives, and spoons
- ☐ 120 paper napkins
- ☐ 16 rolls of paper towels

FOR A FAMILY OF FIVE

For 3 days

- ☐ 15 of each: paper plates, bowls, and cups
- ☐ 15 of each: plastic forks, knives, and spoons
- ☐ 15 paper napkins
- ☐ 2 rolls of paper towels

For 7 days

☐ 35 of each: paper plates, bowls, and cups

☐ 35 of each: plastic forks, knives, and spoons

☐ 35 paper napkins

☐ 4 rolls of paper towels

For 1 month

☐ 150 of each: paper plates, bowls, and cups

☐ 150 of each: plastic forks, knives, and spoons

☐ 150 paper napkins

☐ 16 rolls of paper towels

For cleaning countertops and other surfaces in the kitchen and bathroom and wiping down garbage cans, use disinfectant wipes such as Lysol or Clorox, which claim to kill 99.9 percent of viruses and bacteria. They are not recommended for bare wood surfaces, dishes, glasses, or utensils. I use them periodically to wipe off computer keyboards and mouses, telephone receivers, doorknobs, light switches, remote controls, game sticks, consoles, and other items we handle frequently, and I keep 10 containers on hand at all times.

Disinfectant wipes are an effective and easy way to clean your kitchen or bathroom countertops and small surfaces, but they won't be very useful for a large cleanup job. Also, it's important to have a powerful cleansing agent on hand if the sewer line were to back up or your home were flooded in a storm and lots of bacteria entered your house. To the rescue—common household bleach. I prefer unscented. When using it, first dilute it in water. For mopping tile or linoleum floors, mix 3 ¼ tablespoons (49 ml) of bleach per gallon (3.8 L) of water. To clean countertops, cutting boards, or other surfaces, mix 1 teaspoon (5 ml) of bleach in a gallon (3.8 L) of water. Let the surface air-dry after mopping it or wiping it for best results. Bleach doesn't have a long shelf life, so don't store more than you would use in a year. Handle it with care. You want to avoid getting any in your eyes or mouth or on your clothes, and it can irritate your skin so wear rubber gloves when using it.

By storing just the few simple products I've described here, you'll be prepared for cleanliness in any emergency situation. And that feels really good!

CHAPTER 7
LESSONS IN LAUNDRY

It's been days since the power outage and the piles of laundry grow higher and higher. Everyone in your family is down to his or her last pair of underwear, and there's no sign of relief. Wearing soiled, smelly clothing is not life-threatening, but a little cleanliness can go a long way in lightening the spirit.

In this chapter, I'll share my tried-and-true preparedness plan for dealing with laundry—knowing what to clean and how to clean it. You'll learn to assemble an amazing washer system that requires no electricity and no hand-scrubbing. I'll also share the recipe for homemade laundry detergent that I use all the time. Keeping your family's clothes clean in an emergency will be no source of stress for you.

Stop for a minute and think about the laundry you have piled up around the house. Or maybe you are fortunate to have just folded your last batch of towels. You never know when the power to your washing machine and dryer will be lost because of a disaster or unforeseen emergency. It could be as simple as a car, truck, or train accident that has downed the major power line to your county, city, or neighborhood. If the disaster is severe enough, power might go out at the pump stations that send freshwater through your community's main water line and into your house. All city and county facilities use power to run the sewer treatment facilities, water lines, electric substations, and gas-line pumping sources. And all of them probably have generators to keep systems running for a short time, but eventually the generator fuel will run out.

Hopefully the power outage will last only a few days, if that, but you might find yourself watching the pile in your laundry basket get higher and higher as the emergency drags on and smelling an increasingly pungent aroma from the clothes everyone is wearing. Now is the time to plan ahead and figure out what to do about dirty laundry when power and possibly water are lost in an emergency. At the very least, you'll want clean underwear, right?

STORE THIS ADVICE

If you run out of disposable diapers and don't have any cloth ones on hand, take some old flannel shirts or nightgowns or bathrobes, cut big squares of fabric out of them, and fold them up to make emergency diapers that you secure with safety pins if you don't have diaper pins. You'll also want to cover the diaper with plastic of some sort, perhaps fashioned from a food storage bag.

WATER AND SOAP

You'll notice that almost every chapter in this book starts with a discussion of water. Why? Because it is essential to so many of our day-to-day needs: hydration and health, cooking, washing your hands, brushing your teeth, bathing, cleaning, and, here, washing laundry. That's why my water storage formula—4 gallons (15 L) per person per day—delivers a higher storage recommendation than what you might come across elsewhere. I want to make sure you are well prepared for any emergency. When it comes to doing laundry, my water storage recommendations assume you will only be washing the essentials: underwear, cloth diapers if you need to use them, and family cloths if you run out of toilet paper. If you have a nearby stream, lake, or pool in your backyard, you can use that water to wash clothes even if you don't purify it, and in that case, what and how much laundry you do will be up to your desire and willingness for washing clothes, sheets, and towels by hand in a tub or with a homemade manual washing machine.

GRAY WATER, BLACK WATER

You have probably heard of them: Gray water refers to used sink, tub, shower, and laundry water. Black water is sewer water or any water that has fecal material in it, such as the water used to clean diapers. Neither is potable, meaning you can't drink it, or cook with it. Should your sewer and water systems shut down and become unusable, both should be disposed of at your local gas station if they have a dump station or an RV or campsite dump station. Pouring either gray or black water down your drain could either cause it to back up or possibly contaminate the water system. Wear disposable gloves and follow the rules posted at the station.

HUMAN-POWERED WASHERS

The first electric-powered washing machine was introduced in Chicago in 1908, but humans have been washing clothes for centuries, so when the power cuts out, we modern humans have to revert to some old manual ways of doing our laundry. You can wash underwear by hand in your kitchen sink or with a plastic Japanese Laundry Wash Basin with Washboard, which combines the basin and washboard in one unit. They are only 11 inches (28 cm) wide though so are really only useful for undergarments. If you have water to wash tops, trousers, or other larger pieces of clothing, get a large tub and washboard. I don't recommend washing your clothes in the bathtub, because you'll need to use a lot of water. Also, if the sewer lines are not working, you don't want any water to go down the bathtub drain because it might just come right back up.

Sewer lines can be affected by a number of things, such as coming apart in an earthquake, becoming overburdened by unusually heavy rain and runoff, getting clogged when something that shouldn't be flushed down the toilet does go down. We had a situation a couple of years ago when our local sewer department did some maintenance on the lines and ended up filling the sewer pipe with air pockets. This prevented the sewage from moving through the line and out of our neighborhood, so it backed up and out of our shower drain. The shower, bathtubs, and floor drains are the most common places where sewage shows up if there's a blockage. And if you see any sewage, get out the bleach and your rubber gloves.

If you find out that the sewer lines are clogged, don't put any liquids down your toilets, bathtub, or shower drains. Contaminated water could be stored in buckets or garbage bags until systems are up and running again. Then dispose of them the usual way through the local sewage system. In an extreme or long-term emergency, dumping it in your yard may be the only option available if the area you live in does not have a dump site established. Use common sense on where you dump sewage!

In an emergency, clothes still need to get washed. If it was good enough for grandma, one of these units should be good enough for you.

STORE THIS ADVICE

Those awesome blue jeans you tend to wear most days, won't seem so awesome when you wash them by hand. They are thick, soak up a lot of water, are difficult to wring out, and could take days to dry on the clothesline. If you live in jeans, make sure you have several pair, and think about having a few items in your wardrobe that are easy to wash and wear.

Drill four holes in one bucket.

Gather the Mobile Washer parts and assemble them.

Place the bucket with holes inside the other bucket and use a gamma lid to secure the Mobile Washer.

Add your clothes, water, and detergent to the top bucket and plunge up and down with the Mobile Washer to clean the clothes.

A MOBILE WASHER SYSTEM

The Mobile Washer is a manual washing device that looks very much like a plunger (see illustrations above) and uses a similar action. To use it for cleaning clothes, you'll need two 5- or 6-gallon (19–23-L) buckets (I prefer 6-gallon [23-L]). Put water, detergent, and your clothing in one bucket and plunge the Mobile Washer up and down. This pushes and pulls the soapy water through your clothes to clean them. Next place your clothing into the second bucket filled with clean water and use the Mobile Washer to rinse your clothing.

For more thorough cleaning, I devised a system that uses two buckets stacked one inside the other and a Mobile Washer. The system moves water around a bit more and drains the water when washing is complete. It's simple to build. Here are the items you'll need:

- ☐ A drill
- ☐ A 2-inch (5-cm) drill bit
- ☐ 1 gamma lid
- ☐ Two 6-gallon (23-L) buckets
- ☐ A 1-inch (2.5-cm) drill bit
- ☐ 1 Mobile Washer with handle

(continued)

HERE'S HOW TO PUT IT TOGETHER

1. Drill a 2-inch (5-cm) hole in the center of the gamma lid.
2. Drill four holes in the bottom of one of the buckets with a 1-inch (3-cm) drill bit.
3. Assemble the Mobile Washer according to instructions that came with it.
4. Place the bucket with the holes inside the second bucket.
5. Use a rubber mallet to tap the outer ring of the gamma lid securely onto the top bucket.
6. Place the Mobile Washer in the top bucket, and with the handle of the washer coming up through the 2-inch (5-cm) hole, screw the lid into the ring.

Once the washer is assembled, you are ready to clean. Put clothing, water, and detergent in the top bucket, close the lid, and plunge away. The holes in the top bucket create more friction and water movement, and as you plunge, the dirty water will drain into the bottom bucket. I have two of these systems—one for washing and one for rinsing. I use just ¼ teaspoon of my homemade laundry detergent (below) to 3 gallons (11 L) of water.

One year I gave a set of these to family members and friends as holiday gifts. At first they thought it was the funniest gift ever, but during some of the power outages we've experienced, they put them to use and now see their value.

LAUNDRY DETERGENT

Stock up on a year's worth of your favorite laundry detergent, and you'll be well prepared to clean your clothes through an emergency and even lend some to neighbors and family should they have a need. If you're not sure what a year's worth is, mark the date on your next purchase of detergent and then note the date when it's time to buy more. Then do the math to see how much you'll need for 12 months. Here are two other cleaning agents to consider:

FELS-NAPTHA BARS

These bars of laundry soap have been around for many years and are excellent for removing stains. Squirt a little water on the stain, rub the bar into the fabric, and wash. I like the smell, cleaning efficiency, and price—I've been able to purchase them at under a dollar a bar. You can't go wrong with these. Store a few bars with your laundry supplies.

HOMEMADE LAUNDRY DETERGENT

Until a couple of years ago, I had always bought commercial laundry detergent and fabric softener at the supermarket, and then I discovered that you could make your own, which would work just as well as store-bought brands, if not better, at a fraction of the cost. I made a batch of homemade detergent a few months ago and calculated that it should last me close to eight years based on the amount I use with each load of laundry. I love using this detergent for doing laundry by hand because it creates fewer bubbles, and it's easier to rinse out since it doesn't contain any of the extra fillers that are used to make commercial detergents. The recipe I use calls for the following ingredients, which you can buy at your grocery store:

- ☐ 1 Fels-Naptha bar, grated by hand or in a food processor
- ☐ 1 cup (110 g) borax detergent booster
- ☐ 1 cup (110 g) super washing soda (not baking soda)

To make the detergent, blend all the ingredients together in a blender. I use 1 teaspoon (3 g) per load in my front loader HE (High Efficiency) washing machine and just ¼ teaspoon in a washtub or Mobile Washer.

The cost per load is about 4 cents, depending on the price of the ingredients.

HANGING CLOTHES TO DRY

What gets washed must be dried. Without the convenience of your electricity-driven dryer, you'll need to hang clothes to air-dry. I remember helping my grandmother hang sheets on the clothesline in her yard, and I can still picture those sheets billowing in the wind. You can install a retractable clothesline above the tub in your bathroom, like the ones you see in some hotels, or you can set up an outdoor clothesline. It might be as simple as some line strung between two trees or a slightly more sophisticated setup of lines stretched between two posts. I have one of the umbrella versions that folds up and can be stored in a shed or garage when not in use. These offer an efficient space-saving solution to long straight stretches of clothesline. Think about what option works best for your situation. You might want an outside clothesline as well as an over-the-tub retractable line for drying clothes indoors on cold or rainy days or if a storm is brewing and kicking up a lot of dust or dirt. And be sure to buy sturdy clothespins. My experience is that you get what you pay for. I thought a clothespin was a clothespin, but I bought an inexpensive batch, and the springs fell apart after one use.

Washing clothes by hand and hanging them to dry may not be the most fun thing to do with your time, but if you've ever smelled that clean scent of sheets pulled fresh from the clothesline, you know there's nothing like it.

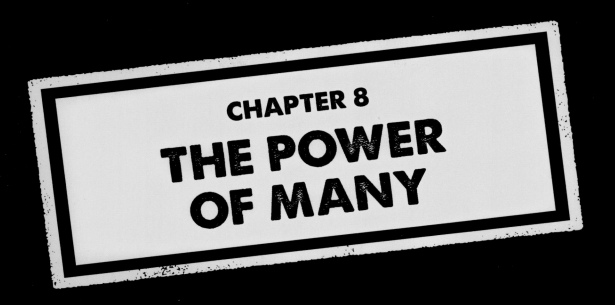

CHAPTER 8

THE POWER OF MANY

Armed with all of the information I've given you about how to prepare for a crisis or what to do if you have to evacuate your home, you know how to take care of yourself and your family. And while you may have great fortitude in the face of disaster, don't do it alone. You don't have to, and what you can accomplish with the help of even one other person is so much greater than what you can do on your own. Tap the power of your family and your neighbors and prepare for hardship together.

In this chapter, I'll help you start the conversation with your family about putting together your emergency plan, and how to approach neighbors to pool resources that will be lifesaving in an emergency. Even if you don't know your neighbors well, I'll give you plenty ideas for how to get acquainted. You will be safer and more comfortable in an emergency knowing you have friends nearby, ready to help each other get through tough situations.

Perhaps the most important resource you have for survival in the face of a crisis isn't water or food or warmth but the people around you—your family, friends, and neighbors. We watched New York City in the immediate aftermath of 9/11. Firefighters, police officers, and everyday citizens aided those who were trapped or injured. People—strangers even—came together, and lives were saved. Hopefully none of us will ever have to face a situation like that in our lives. But even other disasters—earthquakes, hurricanes, tornadoes, floods, fires, or even power outages from ice storms or collapsing infrastructure—are all made easier when family and neighborhoods strive together in the spirit of community to solve problems and plan for emergencies.

FAMILY

Begin your community approach to preparedness at home. Many families have a plan in place in case of a fire, with escape routes and meeting places determined. Perhaps you even have home fire drills in which everyone practices exactly what he or she is supposed to do in a live situation. If you don't have an emergency escape plan, this is a good place to start, and I talk about it in greater detail in Part 2 of this book. In the case of a home fire, you need to determine the best escape route from each room in the house. If you have a two-story home, you may need ladders that attach to the windows and roll down the outside of the house. Then you need to decide where you will all meet once you've left the home. Once you have a plan figured out, bring everyone together and review what each person needs to do. Walk together through the house and point out the escape routes. Explain where you will meet, likely a neighbor's house in this case. And then every so often have a fire drill to practice. When everyone knows what to do, you will function as a team enacting a plan—every person doing their part to reach safety. Preparedness helps prevent panic, and it leads to successful management of an emergency situation.

To make an emergency plan workable for all concerned, you need to get every family member involved.

Involve your family in all of your emergency-preparedness plans because then the responsibility is shared and the execution of your plans will happen more smoothly and successfully. I am going to guess that most of you reading this book have experienced, at the very least, a power outage, if only for a few hours. These days, with so much reliance on electricity to power not only the essentials like the refrigerator but our computers, tablets, and phones, we are quickly inconvenienced by even a blip in power loss. And probably many of you have endured days, a week, maybe more of lost electricity or water because of some natural disaster such as a hurricane. Initiate a discussion among family members by recalling those times and explaining that those kinds of events are becoming more common and your family should be prepared in case your home loses power or water or both in the future. To encourage participation from your kids, consider asking them what they think you need to plan for in case of an emergency. Clean water? Extra food? Light? Heat? Entertainment? Make a list and then tackle some of them together. Your kids' first concern might be the TV and game console. Make a note of it and decide at some point if you want a small generator to power entertainment devices. And speaking of entertainment, though figuring out the essentials—water, food, light, heat—is paramount, don't neglect talking about what your family will enjoy doing if you don't have power for your TV, game console, or computer. Take notes and be sure you plan for fun, too.

In Chapter 2, I suggested sitting down with family members to review what foods and meals they like so that you'll be able to work up a detailed list of what you want to store. Be sure to have your family try those foods in their canned or freeze-dried versions before you buy a whole case. As you start gathering and storing water, food, nonelectric lighting, and other items, ask family members to help you put them in storage so that everyone knows where to find them if and when the lights go out. Practice using your butane stove, and allow those old enough to also try cooking with it. And discuss those first steps to take when you lose power or water or both. When everyone is part of the conversation, even your children, they'll feel ownership of the plan and they'll step up when it's time to get out those lanterns or retrieve the box of blankets from the attic. Also, having a plan and knowing what to do will help you, your spouse, and your children face a crisis with less fear and more calm. And sharing the burdens of handling an emergency will make the challenge easier for everyone to bear.

NEIGHBORS

Getting to know your neighbors and having discussions about emergency preparedness with the other families who live on your street opens up an even greater opportunity to tap into the power of community and combine resources and energy for the benefit of everyone. Think about the many ways you and your neighbors can work together toward preparing for a crisis: you can buy food, water, and other supplies in bulk to get the best prices. You can plant a neighborhood garden and share in harvesting and canning produce. You can create and distribute a list of emergency contacts in the event that a child needs to be picked up at school and his or her parents are stranded at the office. You can do an inventory of tools and skills that might be shared in a disaster—maybe someone has a ham radio that would be useful for communications, or perhaps there's a doctor living on your street who could help in a medical emergency.

By developing relationships in your neighborhood, not only a one-way relationship between your family and every other family on the block but a true community in which everyone knows everyone else, all of you can prepare together as a team for a crisis and you will be able to support each other successfully should one occur. You can gather around a neighbor's hand-cranked radio or generator-driven TV for updates on the current emergency situation. You can share extra resources—that third can opener you had stored, a blanket, or an extra container of wet wipes. You can work together to solve unforeseen problems that may arise. The benefits go on and on including that you'll have many more friends, and friendship is essential to our well-being, crisis or not.

Developing that community takes a little more effort now than it once did. The tight-knit neighborhoods of old seem to have unraveled. We're all so busy. With both parents working to make ends meet financially in many families, the time and opportunity for spontaneous conversations over the fence or for coffee in your neighbor's kitchen seem to have mostly vanished. But getting to know your neighbors, even simply knowing who lives where, the size and ages of families, their general health and mobility, can be invaluable in a crisis.

When my husband and I took the C.E.R.T. class, an important part of the training was learning how to work together as neighbors. We were taught as a team to go door to door—assuming it is safe to do so—to check on how each household dealt with the initial disaster challenges and find out if they are still in the home and doing okay, or, in an evacuation, if the family received the message and followed through.

After the class, I sat down and did an inventory of my neighborhood, including the homes on both sides of the street and going at least 10 houses in both directions—a total of 20 families. I found there were a number of people I didn't know well, or at all—which made me feel sad. I determined to do a better job of neighboring. I came up with an approach that I hoped would work for most of us as we tried to become better neighbors. I took a stack of 3 x 5 inch (8 x 13 cm) index cards and typed on them my name and my husband's, our address, our home phone number, both of our cell phone numbers, and both of our e-mail addresses. I also included information for two of my daughters who don't live near me and whom I would want my neighbors to contact in an emergency. Then I went door to door and handed the cards out, introducing myself to those I didn't know. I suggested that, if they felt comfortable doing so, they might create similar cards to pass around in the neighborhood so that we'd all know how to get in touch with each other if a need should arise.

Our neighborhood has become so much closer as a result. Not long after we began sharing our contact information, our area experienced a torrential storm, and several homes were flooded with water and mud. Some swimming pools were filled with orange-brown muddy water. The rocky, rugged terrain here is beautiful and provides wonderful opportunities for hiking, rock climbing, and rappelling, but when we have a sudden downpour, it can be very dangerous. During the flooding, neighbors were texting each other to make sure everyone was okay and to ask if anyone needed anything. It was very reassuring to witness that response and to know that my husband and I are not alone in a crisis and that others are just down the street ready and willing to lend a helping hand.

I've spoken throughout this book about the importance of being prepared so that you can take care of yourself and your family in an emergency situation, and there's a certain sense of security that comes with preparedness, it feels good to know you can handle the aftermath of a disaster. But it's further reassuring and comforting to have good relationships with your neighbors and to know that come what may—a fire, a tornado, a hurricane, a flood, an earthquake, or simply a torrential rainstorm—you will share labor, tools, and know-how and face the situation together.

STORE THIS ADVICE

See if you can talk your neighbors into getting some walkie talkies. The perfect neighborhood solution when landlines and cell service fail. Experts recommend Motorola Talkabout 2-Way Radios #MR350R. If you purchase them as a group you will all have the same model and can set them to the same channel. Plus, you might get a discount.

A DOZEN WAYS TO GET TO KNOW YOUR NEIGHBORS

I have said many times when I teach emergency preparedness classes, "That guy down the street with the chain saw may become your new best friend." We also need to get to know the elderly or physically handicapped individuals in our neighborhoods who might need help even in some nonemergency circumstances. If you don't feel quite comfortable knocking on doors of the homes up and down your street, introducing yourself, and handing out your contact information on index cards as I did, there are many ways that you can begin to meet your neighbors and build relationships so that down the road you can share phone numbers and e-mails and have conversations about emergency preparedness. Here are several ideas:

1. When getting the mail from your mailbox, say hello to your neighbors if they're outdoors as well.
2. Plan a neighborhood movie night and offer to make the popcorn.
3. Invite friends and neighbors over to play cards around your table or horseshoes in the backyard.
4. Plan a potluck dinner or barbecue and have people bring their favorite dish along with the recipe to share.

Neighbors can become more than just friends in an emergency; they can be part of a larger community support team.

5. Suggest having a girls' night out or a luncheon to get to know each other.

6. If you have kids, plan playdates, join the local PTA, or volunteer to coach a youth team.

7. Consider joining a local church and volunteering on a committee.

8. Organize a block party and recruit some neighbors to help you.

9. Get a dog. People often can't resist saying hello or stopping to talk when they come upon someone walking his or her dog down the street.

10. If you make bread or jam take a loaf or a jar to a neighbor as a way of introducing yourself. Offer your contact information in case of emergency. Most likely your neighbor will reciprocate by sharing his or her contact information with you.

11. Spend more time in your front yard or on your porch or balcony. It creates an opportunity to say hello to those passing by on foot or bicycle.

12. Encourage a community of mutual concern. Pay attention to what's going on in your neighborhood. If you see a garage door open at night when it's usually closed, alert the home owner. If you suspect that the door-to-door solicitor who stopped by may be casing homes for possible burglary, alert your neighbors. If newspapers are piling up on someone's front porch or the grass hasn't been mowed in a while, call on that person to make sure everything is okay. As you show concern for those around you, others will model your behavior, and you'll create a neighborhood culture of mutual respect and support.

Once you've established relationships with neighbors, start the conversation about emergency preparedness. Talk about what you're doing and why, and learn what others are doing or not doing. They may look to you for advice. And as it feels right, discuss how you can pool your resources—labor, skills, and purchasing power—to prepare for and then handle a crisis situation—together.

PART II
WHEN YOU NEED TO BUG OUT

* * *

HOW TO PREPARE FOR AN EVACUATION

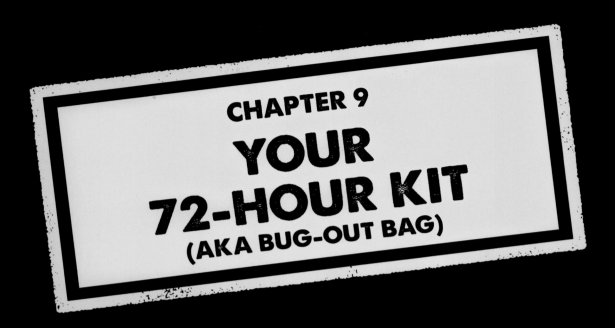

CHAPTER 9
YOUR 72-HOUR KIT
(AKA BUG-OUT BAG)

Your home's fire alarms blare in the night and everyone is awakened from a deep sleep. You smell smoke and hear the crackling of flames. Everyone needs to get out immediately. A house fire, wildfire, hurricane, tornado, landslide, flooding, possibly the threat of a terrorist attack—there are any number of crises that could force you and your family to evacuate your home. Are you prepared?

In this chapter, you'll learn what a 72-Hour Kit is and how to put one together for every member of your family, including children, babies, and even your pets. I'll tell you what the essentials are that you need to have, then suggest other items that will make life easier if you have room for them in your pack. You'll also learn about keeping a kit at the office, in case you're at work when disaster strikes. These packs will be lifesavers if your family needs to evacuate, and you'll sleep soundly at night knowing nothing important will be left behind if you need to get out fast.

During the 1980s, my husband and I lived in a small community north of Salt Lake City called Farmington. One winter the snowstorms were fierce, filling the mountain snowpack to depths the locals hadn't seen in decades. Our community was laid out just at the foot of the Wasatch Mountains and between two streams that flowed from the canyons. The local government officials warned us that if there were a quick thaw, those streams would become rivers and put many homes in jeopardy. They suggested that every family start planning ahead and stock 72-hour-kits in case we had to evacuate to the local church or school.

Sure enough, after experiencing one of the heaviest snowfalls in close to 100 years, the spring temperatures were unseasonably warm. The streams gained volume and speed, and families were told to keep their children away from the banks of the rushing water. After a few days, we thought we were going to be okay, then one night it rained up in the mountains and that sent everything toppling. The streams overflowed, pushing water, mud, and boulders the size of small cars into the community. Families living near the water were asked to evacuate to the nearby church. Although my family lived a safe distance from the heart of the disaster we grabbed our 72-hour kits and hurried to the church to see if we could help. Though only about 15 homes were affected directly by the flood, close to a 100 families showed up at the church.

In the aftermath of the disaster, as life settled back to normal, our local authorities conducted a follow-up meeting to evaluate how emergency responders as well as the residents had performed during the crisis. To most everyone's amazement only a couple of families had brought 72-hour kits, and none of them were families whose homes had been destroyed by the flooding. Every emergency agency in the country recommends having a 72-hour kit available in the event of an evacuation. That night, I made a renewed commitment to having a kit for each member of my family, ready to grab and go at a moment's notice.

I've read so many stories of families forced out of their apartments or homes under various emergency circumstances, and I am sure you have, too. Hurricanes Katrina and Sandy come to mind immediately. Wildfires seem to rage every summer in California, and we read about floods, landslides, and chemical spills or broken gas lines that necessitate evacuation. These incidents are happening more frequently as our climate changes and our country's infrastructure ages under a lack of maintenance. I always wonder when hearing about these crises, if the families who were forced to leave their homes were able to take any essentials with them.

Every family, every individual is unique, and each of us could approach gathering our must-have belongings differently, but there are several essential items that every person, regardless of age or sex, needs to pack in case you must leave your home in an emergency—essentials such as water, food, and prescription medications. Over the next several pages I'll provide a list of items to pack in 72-hour kits that fulfill the needs of adults, children, babies, and even pets for a 3-day (72-hour) time period. I'll also discuss briefly how your place of work might want to prepare for a possible evacuation. Having a 72-hour kit—also called a grab-and-go bag or bug-out bag—ready and accessible is reassuring, and it reduces the panic in an emergency. There'll be no scrambling to locate and gather essential items before you and your family leave your house. This would be the time to grab that binder full of your important documents (discussed in more detail in Chapter 10).

AN ADULT KIT

One day while doing an inventory of what I had in my husband's and my 72-hour kit, I decided to sit down and write out a wish list of the things I'd want if we were ever evacuated and expected to survive outside our home for three days. That list became rather lengthy. It included several items that would be convenient to have but not necessary, and I realized I couldn't fit everything I wanted inside our kits. So I've created two lists, which you'll find below. The first highlights the essentials that every kit should contain. The second is a compilation of items that could come in handy in an emergency situation. After you've packed the essentials, if you have room to fit a few more items—and can physically carry more—review the additional suggestions and add anything that you feel might make your emergency journey easier.

When I first heard about needing a 72-hour kit, I was a young mom and accustomed to carrying a diaper bag around with me everywhere my family went. I figured I'd just buy a bigger diaper bag, stuff it with supplies, and we'd be ready to go. As I learned about what items a family should take with them in an evacuation, I realized an oversized diaper bag wasn't going to cut it. So start by purchasing a large, sturdy backpack—one with wheels that you can use as a roller bag in case it is too heavy. If you need to buy several backpacks for your family and there's no room in your budget, you can store supplies in clearly marked boxes or heavy-duty transparent garbage bags—because you don't want to accidentally put your 72-hour kits out for trash pickup. Collect your supplies bit by bit and consider putting foods that need to be rotated in baggies to make it easy to find them and switch them out with fresh replacements. Be mindful of items that might leak or break open—zippered plastic bags are a good solution. I also recommend attaching three tags to your kit with the following information:

1. Your name and phone numbers
2. A reminder to grab your prescription medications
3. A reminder to take your emergency binder (see Chapter 10)
4. Your photo on the bag of the tag so a stranger can identify the bag as yours if for whatever reason you are not conscious

Be sure to update your kit every six months to a year, depending on the items you have in it.

STORE THIS ADVICE

You can purchase prepacked 72-hour kits online. You will need to add food and water and a few other items based on your preferences, but this is an easy way to get started.

THE ESSENTIALS

Here are the necessary items to include in a 72-hour kit for one adult.

- [ ] Water—You'll need one 3.5-gallon (13-L) Water Brick filled with water (it weighs approximately 29 pounds [13 kg]), which has a handle for carrying, plus a Sport Berkey Bottle or similar water purifier that you can put in your backpack.

- [ ] Food—Pack what you like to eat and foods that are energy dense (a lot of calories in a small volume, such as granola bars or nuts). I recommend purchasing primarily freeze-dried foods since they are much lighter to carry and you can eat them right out of the container for convenience. Here's a suggested list of food items to include in your kit (note: servings of instant and freeze-dried foods are based on Thrive products).

  - [ ] Cereal, 3 packages of instant oatmeal or single-serving boxed cereal

  - [ ] Instant milk, 1 pantry can provides 18 servings

  - [ ] Fruits, freeze-dried, 2 pouches provides about 12 servings

  - [ ] Vegetables, freeze-dried, 1 pantry can provides 13 to 16 servings depending on the veggie you choose

  - [ ] Protein, freeze-dried chopped chicken, 1 pantry can provides 7 servings

  - [ ] 6 snacks (2 per day), such as granola or protein bars, nuts, trail mix, chocolate

- [ ] Blanket, Mylar

- [ ] Cash—$100, if possible, in fives and ones, plus 1 roll each of quarters, dimes, nickels, and pennies. This can also be placed in the emergency binder, discussed on page 164.

- [ ] Two photos of everyone you are traveling with, along with your contact information, in case you get separated and need to post a missing-person photo on an emergency bulletin board. These can also be placed in the emergency binder, discussed on page 153.

- [ ] A photocopy of your driver's license in case you run out the door without your wallet or purse. This can also be placed in the emergency binder, discussed on page 153.

- [ ] A contact list with the names and phone numbers of everyone you are traveling with as well as names and phone numbers of family members or friends whom you would want emergency responders to call if you were seriously injured or worse.

- [ ] Compass

- [ ] Can opener

- [ ] First-aid kit that is small enough to fit in your 72-hour bag or kit. Make sure it includes essentials like Band-Aids and antiseptic ointment.

- [ ] Flashlight, preferably battery-free with hand crank and solar chargeable

- [ ] Mess kit

- [ ] Wet wipes, a 24-count pack

- [ ] Tissues, 3 packs of the travel size

- [ ] Toothbrush

It's surprising how much you can pack into a quality adult 72-hour kit. Plan ahead and be selective in deciding what needs to be included.

- ☐ Toothpaste, travel-size tube
- ☐ Shampoo, travel-size bottle
- ☐ Feminine hygiene products for three days, if applicable
- ☐ Whistle
- ☐ Gloves, one pair, non-latex
- ☐ Garbage bags—3 (33-gallon [125-L]) heavy-duty black garbage bags and 3 (13-gallon [49-L]) bags
- ☐ N-95 mask, three
- ☐ All purpose knife, like a Leatherman or Swiss Army
- ☐ Duct tape, one roll
- ☐ Matches, waterproof
- ☐ Extra charger for your phone
- ☐ Extra contact lenses and cleaning solution

NONESSENTIALS

When you leave your house, you are heading into the unknown. In a planned evacuation, you will be asked to go to a specific destination, a church, school, possibly a Y where there should be supplies to help support you and others during the 72 hours after disaster has struck and beyond, but you won't know exactly what you'll find until you get there. Here are several items that might come in handy at your evacuation destination. Clearly you won't fit them all in your 72-hour kit, though if you have room in your car, you could store many of these tools and supplies there. Review the list and consider adding those items that you feel you'd like to have with you and that will fit in your bug-out bag.

- ☐ Over-the-counter medications such as aspirin, ibuprofen, naproxen, vitamins, cold remedies, antacids, Imodium (antidiarrhea medicine), etc.
- ☐ Batteries (all sizes, rotate yearly)
- ☐ Bee sting and snakebite kit
- ☐ Bible/scriptures
- ☐ Birth control
- ☐ Bleach, unscented
- ☐ Books for young and old
- ☐ Bug spray
- ☐ Bung wrench/Gas shut-off wrench
- ☐ Candles or glow sticks
- ☐ Cards or small games to play
- ☐ Coats, jackets, sweaters, extra clothes, shoes
- ☐ Coffeepot and coffee or instant coffee
- ☐ Cooking pot, griddle or fry pan

(continued)

- [ ] Cotton swabs
- [ ] Dish towels and dish soap
- [ ] Emergency travel sewing kit
- [ ] Eyeglasses, extra pair
- [ ] Fingernail clippers and nail file
- [ ] Fire extinguisher
- [ ] Hand warmers
- [ ] Hairbrush and/or comb
- [ ] Hat, gloves, and/or scarf
- [ ] Headlamp
- [ ] Hearing aid, plus batteries
- [ ] Ipecac
- [ ] Kelly Kettle, which you can use to boil water or cook foods using even dried grass for fuel (needs matches)
- [ ] Lantern or compact light
- [ ] Lip balm
- [ ] Mirror
- [ ] Pencils and pens
- [ ] Petroleum jelly
- [ ] Pillow
- [ ] Plastic food-storage bags, all sizes
- [ ] Radio, hand-crank or battery-powered, plus extra batteries
- [ ] Rain poncho
- [ ] Rope
- [ ] Safety pins, several sizes
- [ ] Scissors
- [ ] Solar lights
- [ ] Sticky notes, which come in handy if you need to move from one location to another and being able to leave a note for friends or family would be essential
- [ ] Sunglasses
- [ ] Tent
- [ ] Thermal underwear
- [ ] Thermometer
- [ ] Tools (hammer, screwdrivers, wrench, and a foldable shovel and axe)
- [ ] Umbrella
- [ ] Walkie Talkies (test their range so you know the distance at which they'll work). These are great to have. Experts recommend Motorola Talkabout 2-Way Radios #MR350R.

GRAB-AND-GO BEDSIDE BAG

You are awakened in the middle of the night by your smoke alarms or emergency sirens and you quickly realize your family needs to get out of the house. It's dark, you don't have any shoes on, and you'll need the keys to the car. With this in mind, I created emergency bags to hold keys, a flashlight, shoes, socks, and a list of what you need to grab on the way out: 72-hour kits, your emergency binder, and prescription medications. It's a simple design that uses a pillowcase folded into thirds and then sewn to create pockets. I leave a flap at the top of the bag, which fits nicely between the mattress and box spring of my bed, allowing the bag to hang at my bedside, so I can quickly and easily grab it and go (see the illustrations below for making this pouch). Make one for every member of your family. I recommend staging the occasional drill so your kids can practice exactly what they need to do in a real emergency. Have family members get into bed (with their shoes off). Turn out the lights, and then signal for everyone to get up, grab the items in their bedside bag, and meet in the backyard.

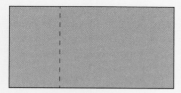

1. Use a pencil to divide a standard-size pillowcase in thirds.

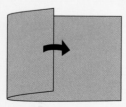

2. Fold over one third.

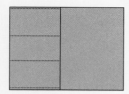

3. By hand or with a machine, sew along the edges and make three pockets.

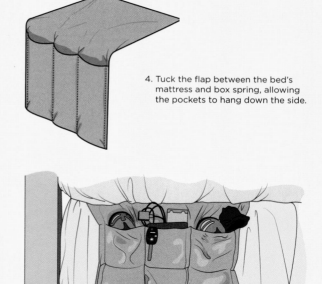

4. Tuck the flap between the bed's mattress and box spring, allowing the pockets to hang down the side.

5. Fill the pockets with emergency supplies, and you'll be thankful to have essential items at hand during a power outage, evacuation, or other emergency.

A CHILD'S KIT

Children need their own 72-hour kit to meet their specific dietary needs, hygiene, and comfort, and you'll want to pack some books and games to keep them occupied during long stretches of time or to help distract them if the situation seems scary. I suggest the same backpack with wheels for children that I recommend for adults. The wheels allow kids to pull the bag behind them. Attach a tag with your child's name and your phone numbers. If your child takes special medications or prescriptions, add a tag with a reminder note to grab those medicines on your way out the door.

THE ESSENTIALS

Pack the following items in a 72-hour kit for one child:

- ☐ Water, one 3.5-gallon (13-L) Water Brick and a Berkey Sport Bottle (the Water Brick will need to be carried separately by a parent)
- ☐ Food, three days' worth; amounts will depend on the age of your child. Also, kids tend to be pickier eaters than adults. Choose foods they'll eat. Here are some suggestions:
  - ☐ Cereal, instant oatmeal or single-serving boxes
  - ☐ Fruit, freeze-dried or single-serving fruit cups or applesauce
  - ☐ Vegetables, freeze-dried
  - ☐ Freeze-dried yogurt bites
  - ☐ Peanut butter
  - ☐ Crackers
  - ☐ Tuna
  - ☐ Trail mix
  - ☐ Pudding, single servings
  - ☐ Granola bars or cereal bars
  - ☐ Ramen noodles or instant soups (assuming you will be able to heat water)
- ☐ Diapers and diaper rash ointment if needed for a baby or toddler
- ☐ Wet wipes, a 24-count pack
- ☐ Blanket, Mylar
- ☐ Baby bottle or a mess kit for a toddler or older child
- ☐ Fever-reducing medicine such as Children's Motrin or Children's Tylenol and any over-the-counter medications your child may need
- ☐ N-95 masks, 3, size appropriate
- ☐ Photo of child and parent in case you are separated with names and contact info written on the back
- ☐ Extra clothing, socks, underwear, and shoes
- ☐ Books, puzzles, coloring books and crayons, and games that your child enjoys

A MOMMY MINI KIT

My husband and I don't have any little ones living with us anymore, our daughters are grown with children of their own, so I asked them and other young mothers in my neighborhood what baby items they would want to take with them in an evacuation. Based on their responses I took one of my spare metal ammo boxes and started filling it with baby and toddler items to create a mommy mini kit. As mothers, we have so many things to remember that having this kit ready and stored in the car means one less thing to have to worry about in an emergency. Of course, you would fill your kit with the most important items for the ages of your children or grandchildren, but here are some suggestions:

- ☐ Diapers (disposable as well as cloth), safety pins, and waterproof pants for three days. The amounts will vary depending on the age of your child, but the average is about 10 disposable or cloth diapers a day. Safety pins for cloth diapers should only require one set, but having two in case one broke or was lost is recommended. You'll need one fresh pair of rubber pants a day at minimum.
- ☐ Diaper rash ointment
- ☐ Underwear
- ☐ Water, 6 Blue Cans—it's safe to store these in your car and when shaken, they chill a little bit
- ☐ Favorite child snacks—choose those that won't leak or melt
- ☐ Baby nail clippers
- ☐ Baby lotion and possibly baby sunscreen
- ☐ Baby liquid soap
- ☐ Baby bottle
- ☐ Baby powder
- ☐ Baby shampoo
- ☐ Baby wipes
- ☐ Pacifiers
- ☐ Baby Motrin

PET KIT

When it comes to creating 72-hour kits, don't forget your pets. You'll want to take them along in an evacuation, and they'll need food and water, too. For your dog or cat, pack the following essentials:

- ☐ Water for 3 days, calculate 1 ounce (30 ml) of water per pound (454 g) of body weight per day
- ☐ Food for 3 days
- ☐ Dishes for food and water
- ☐ Leash or harness
- ☐ Two photos of your pet(s) with your contact information in case you get separated and need to post a missing-pet photo on an emergency bulletin board

OTHER ITEMS TO CONSIDER

- ☐ Complete medical records
- ☐ Chip ID information
- ☐ Sweater
- ☐ Toys
- ☐ Blanket
- ☐ Brush/comb
- ☐ Pet first-aid book
- ☐ Vet wrap 2-inch and 4-inch (5- and 10-cm)/ trauma pad
- ☐ Gauze bandage rolls (2 inch [5 cm], 4 inch [10 cm], and 6 inch [15 cm])
- ☐ Adhesive tape
- ☐ Tweezers
- ☐ Scissors
- ☐ Surgical soap
- ☐ Thermometer and mineral oil
- ☐ Disinfectant solution
- ☐ Styptic powder/cornstarch
- ☐ Benadryl/triple antibiotic ointment
- ☐ Eyewash
- ☐ Saline
- ☐ Medications, 5-day supply
- ☐ Flea and tick treatment
- ☐ Paper towels, one roll

- ☐ Plastic bags and ziplock bags for waste disposal
- ☐ Dog and/or cat carrier(s)
- ☐ Cat-litter box and litter

If you have reptiles, birds, hamsters, or other pets, you'll need to pack a little 72-hour kit for them too. Know this: Red Cross Centers only allow service animals, they will not accept your pets.

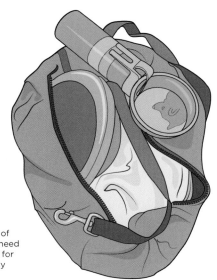

Pets are an important part of the family. We need to be prepared for their emergency care, too.

AT THE OFFICE

Don't leave home without it—an EDC (Every Day Carry) Bag. These come in various styles: sling backpacks, messenger-type bags, and a version that looks like a tool belt and attaches to your pants belt and around your thigh. They're great for carrying items that would be useful in an emergency situation at the office or on the road. Below is a list of the things that I store in my EDC. You might add to this list.

- ☐ Multi-tool knife
- ☐ Hand sanitizer
- ☐ Mirror (If stranded, you can flash it to alert people to your location.)
- ☐ Compass
- ☐ Whistle
- ☐ Small bills (fives and ones) and coins
- ☐ Water bottle with a filter such as the Sport Berkey Bottle

- ☐ Small first-aid kit
- ☐ Duct tape, small roll
- ☐ Seat belt cutter
- ☐ Flashlight and extra batteries
- ☐ Pen and small paper tablet
- ☐ Folding knife
- ☐ USB charger for phones and tablets
- ☐ Aspirin and benadryl
- ☐ Pepper spray

BUSINESS EMERGENCY PREPAREDNESS

Your company should have an evacuation plan in case of an emergency, and you've likely participated in the occasional fire drill. Medium- to large-size companies usually are well-prepared for emergencies with sprinkler systems, fire extinguishers, generators, emergency lighting, data backup and so forth, but if you work for a small firm, you might want to inquire about emergency preparedness and initiate a discussion about how your company can plan for a disaster that forces employees to evacuate as well as one that requires all employees to stay at the office for a period of time until it is safe to leave. And remember, the first priority is always drinking water.

Once you've stocked all the 72-hour kits your family will need, put them and the Water Bricks in a place where you can easily grab them on your way out the door, such as a closet near the main entrance to your home. An ideal option would be to store your kits in a sheltered place outside the home that doesn't experience extreme heat or cold, and then that becomes your designated meeting place in an evacuation. If you have no storage place outside, your only option is to store it in a closet, under a bed, or behind a couch. With bug-out bags ready to roll, you can sleep in peace, knowing your family is prepared to escape disaster at a moment's notice.

STATE OF MAINE
CERTIFICATE OF BIRTH

SOCIAL SECURITY

...ith

DEBIT
CARD

Mishanter
Financial

Martin Smith

9867 5468 9786 1245

98675468   97 86 12

CHAPTER 10

ESSENTIAL DOCUMENTS:
DON'T LEAVE HOME WITHOUT THEM

When a fire, hurricane, landslide, or earthquake forces you to evacuate your home, you clear out not knowing if your house will be there when you return. Don't leave your critical documents behind to possibly perish with everything else you own. I have a simple solution for taking all the paper and data necessary for day-to-day life management with you.

In this chapter, you'll put together an emergency document binder with essential information. If you need to get out of your home quick, all you'll have to do is grab the binder and you've got all your important documents, along with cash and other items that you'll need in an emergency.

One Christmas, a friend's son was working on his motorcycle in the family's garage and using a space heater to stay warm. The motorcycle's fuel line came loose, gas sprayed all over the floor and walls of the garage, and the space heater soon set the fuel on fire. Fortunately the son was able to get out safely, but the garage was quickly engulfed in flames that spread to the rafters and into the main house. Firefighters were able to put out the fire, but not without having to cut holes in the roof of the house to get to the blaze in the rafters. The family lost one of their cars, four motorcycles, a garage full of tools, and so many of their household items, including Christmas presents ready to be enjoyed. Dense smoke had filled the house, and water was everywhere. Major cleanup and repairs needed to be completed before the family could return home, and they were stranded without essential documents—insurance policies and accounts, banking information, as well as phone numbers for all of the key account holders they would need to reach as they worked to recover from the devastation. It was a nightmare that could have been avoided if they had been able to take all that critical information with them as they headed out the door.

In the aftermath of disaster, the stories I hear from families have one thing in common: They wished they had taken with them contact information for key professionals—lawyers, insurance agents, bankers, doctors—insurance and bank account information, passwords, Social Security cards, some cash, and other documents and data that have become so integral to our lives.

In the midst of a disaster or emergency the logical and natural response to the situation is to protect our family by securing those things that support life—water, food, and shelter. Once the crisis is over, we are thrilled to have survived, but shortly thereafter, we are faced with the reality that we have to piece back together life as we once knew it. To do that, we need access to money to be able to purchase the basics—food, water, and clothing—and pay for repairs to our house. We need to contact our insurance agent to check coverage and begin the process of assessing damage. Perhaps someone in the family needs follow-up medical care that requires your health insurance card.

Putting together a binder with important documents takes some work, but it is well worth your efforts now, before an emergency occurs.

By now you've assembled—or plan to assemble—a 72-hour kit with food, water, and supplies that your family will need for three days; you also need to gather and organize life's essential documents in one place that makes it easy for you to grab them on the way out of your house in an evacuation, and that best place to store your info is an emergency binder or what I like to call a Grab-and-Go Binder. Mine is a simple three-ring notebook with tabs to categorize and identify the different information and documents I want to have on hand and formatted content pages to make it simple to collect and record key contacts, phone numbers, account numbers, and so forth. You can purchase these pages in a downloadable PDF for a small fee from my website (foodstoragemoms.com/shop/emergency-binder-printables). Now let's review tab by tab what documents and data you should include in your binder.

TAB #1: EMERGENCY CONTACT INFORMATION AND PHOTO POCKETS

You may think you've memorized all of the phone numbers that are most important to you, or you feel confident that they're stored in your smartphone, tablet, or laptop. And perhaps that's the case, but in times of stress, your memory may falter, and depending on the crisis, you may not have cell phone or Internet connection. What's your backup? An emergency contact information sheet. Start by writing down the names of everyone who lives with you, his or her cell, and the phone numbers of all possible places where he or she might be when disaster strikes: work, school, a neighbor's house, a volunteer organization, gym, a sports team practice, wherever. Next, add contact information for the following individuals and organizations:

☐ Family members who don't live with you and whom you'd like to call to let them know what's happened and how you're doing

☐ Your employer's work, home, and cell number so you can inform him or her of your situation

☐ Your close neighbors who will want to know your status and how to reach you

☐ Doctors

☐ Local police

☐ Fire department

☐ Ambulance service

☐ Utilities such as gas, electric, or water

☐ Poison control, in case you or a loved one has accidentally ingested something that is or may be poisonous

☐ Your lawyer if you have one

PHOTO POCKETS

C.E.R.T training teaches that we should all have two photos of every family member in our binders: one to keep in your possession and the other to provide to any agency requesting it for purposes of locating or identifying your spouse or child in case you have become separated. I recommend putting these photos on a flash drive so they can be reproduced if necessary.

STORE THIS ADVICE

You definitely want a printed version of your emergency information and documents because you simply won't know whether or not you'll have access to power. Still, consider scanning insurance cards, birth certificates, photo IDs, and other essential items and downloading them along with the pages from your emergency binder to a flash drive.

EMERGENCY CONTACT INFORMATION

NAME	PHONE NUMBER(S)	ADDRESS AND/OR EMAIL ADDRESS
FIRST CONTACT: Relationship:		
Other Contact: Relationship:		
Other Contact: Relationship:		
Other Contact: Relationship:		
Other Contact: Relationship:		
Other Contact: Relationship:		
Other Contact: Relationship:		
WORK CONTACT:		
NEIGHBOR:		
DOCTOR:		
POLICE:	Emergency: Nonemergency:	
FIRE DEPARTMENT:	Emergency: Nonemergency:	
AMBULANCE:	Emergency: Nonemergency:	
GAS COMPANY:	Emergency: Nonemergency:	
ELECTRIC COMPANY:	Emergency: Nonemergency:	
WATER COMPANY:	Emergency: Nonemergency:	
POISON CONTROL	Emergency: Nonemergency:	

TAB #2: BANK AND INVESTMENT ACCOUNTS

If you have to reconstruct your financial situation after a disaster, it will be much easier with a list of all of your bank and investment accounts, loans, credit cards, and so forth. As you build this list include the name, address, and phone number of the institution that holds your account as well as the account number. Start with the checking and savings accounts for every individual you live with. My husband and I have separate checking accounts and we both own home-based businesses that each have their own accounts. Here is a list of others to consider adding to your list:

☐ Retirement accounts, including IRAs and 401(k)s

☐ Bank credit cards such as VISA, MasterCard, American Express, and Discover

☐ Store credit cards, such as Macy's, JCPenney, Nordstrom, and Sears

☐ I suggest you make copies of the front and back of all your cards so you not only have the card numbers for reference, but also the instructions on what to do in case of loss.

☐ Investment accounts such as those you might have with Charles Schwab, Merrill Lynch, or other investment companies. Include your broker's name and contact information as well.

☐ 529 college savings plans

☐ If you have individual stock certificates or bonds with coupons to be clipped you may be wise to write the certificate numbers down in your binder as well.

BANK CONTACT INFORMATION

BANK NAME	ACCOUNT NUMBER	PHONE NUMBER AND/OR EMAIL ADDRESS	BUSINESS ADDRESS

TAB #3: CRITICAL DOCUMENTS

For this section of the binder, use a plastic insert with a pocket or a zippered bag that you can attach to the rings inside your notebook. Store originals or copies of the life documents that you keep in a safety deposit box at your bank, such as birth certificates for you, your spouse, and your children. Here are some other possibilities:

- ☐ Your will
- ☐ Living wills for yourself and your family members
- ☐ Marriage license and prenuptial agreement if one exists
- ☐ Adoption papers, if appropriate
- ☐ Diplomas
- ☐ Special licensing certificates
- ☐ Trademark or copyright documentation
- ☐ Religious certificates such as baptism, bar mitzvah, confirmation
- ☐ If you were in the military you may want to include induction papers, certificates of retirement points earned, discharge papers, VA benefit qualification papers, and so forth.
- ☐ If you own a business you may want to include organizational papers, copies of company stock certificates, and partnership agreements.
- ☐ If you're divorced, you may want to have copies of the divorce decree and any subsequent amendments.

You may think I'm going overboard here, but you can't assume that the bank where you have these documents safely stored will be open, or that it will even exist, after a major disaster. It may be that the only copies of documents critical to your future will be the ones in your binder. I actually store my binder in a fireproof safe.

TAB #4: FREQUENTLY REFERENCED DOCUMENTS AND ID CARDS

This tab is where I place those important documents and cards that my family uses regularly such as driver's licenses and insurance cards. You could include them under tab #3 but I feel that since you need them more frequently, you should give them their own place in your binder for easier access. With some of these items—your driver's license, for example—you'll want to carry the original in a wallet or purse, so make copies to include in your binder. Consider storing the following items in this tab if you have them.

- ☐ Passports
- ☐ Social Security card
- ☐ Medicare or Medicaid cards
- ☐ Health insurance cards
- ☐ Concealed weapons permits
- ☐ Military retirement forms
- ☐ Gym or recreation center passes or card
- ☐ Library cards
- ☐ Loyalty cards for grocery stores, restaurants, movie theaters, or other retail businesses

INSURANCE CONTACT INFORMATION

COMPANY INFORMATION	PHONE NUMBER	POLICY NUMBER
Health Insurance: Agent:		
Health Insurance: Agent:		
Dental Insurance: Agent:		
Eye Insurance: Agent:		
Life Insurance: Agent:		
Life Insurance: Agent:		
Auto Insurance: Agent:		
Long-Term Care Insurance: Agent:		
Home Insurance: Agent:		

MEDICARE INFORMATION

MEDICARE INSURANCE TYPE	
Medicare A	
Medicare B	
Medicare C	
Medicare D	

TAB #5: MEDICAL AND DENTAL INFORMATION

Having all your medical information with you can be critical in an emergency, and I don't just mean the phone numbers of your doctors, dentist, and insurance companies. If something should happen that renders you unconscious or unable to speak to emergency responders, you'll want them to have a record of any current health issues and the medications that you're taking so that they can administer an appropriate treatment that won't cause a life-threatening reaction. Having your medical information in your emergency binder could save your life. Though I've suggested including your doctors' and dentist's contact information in the first tab, it doesn't hurt to repeat them here in case this is the first section of the binder you turn to in a medical situation. For that same reason, I suggest including copies of your health insurance or Medicare or Medicaid cards here as well as under tab #4.

For each member of your family, create a personal health history that includes the following details:

☐ Current and chronic health issues such as diabetes, high blood pressure, high cholesterol, or other cardiovascular disease, any type of seizures, Parkinson's, MS, any health problem that requires ongoing treatment and possibly medication.

☐ All allergies, including reactions to medications.

☐ All prescriptions that you or family members take, along with dosing information.

☐ All supplements that you or family members use regularly, including calcium, fish oil or omega-3s, vitamin E, and other vitamins or minerals, along with the dose that you are taking. We tend to assume supplements are harmless, but some can cause serious complications when taken with certain prescription medications.

☐ Be sure to note if you are pregnant since it may not be obvious.

☐ It can also be helpful to include a general medical history of your parents, grandparents, and siblings. Knowing what health problems your extended family suffered can give medical providers a better picture of your condition. This is important information to have regardless of an emergency.

Update this information at least every 12 months to make sure it is current.

MEDICAL INFORMATION

PATIENT INFORMATION		
Name:	Date of Birth:	SS:
		Home: Cell:
Name:	Date of Birth:	SS:
		Home: Cell:
Name:	Date of Birth:	SS:
		Home: Cell:
Name:	Date of Birth:	SS:
		Home: Cell:

DOCTOR	PHONE NUMBER

DENTIST	PHONE NUMBER

PHARMACY	PHONE NUMBER

NAME	MEDICAL CONDITIONS/ ALLERGIES TO MEDICATIONS/FOODS

NAME	MEDICATION	DOSAGE AMOUNTS	FREQUENCY

NAME	PREVIOUS SURGERIES	DATE OF SURGERY

TAB #6: WEBSITE ACCESS INFORMATION

As I've worked with people to set up their binders, I've discovered that in many families, everybody's doing their own thing online and that there are multiple accounts and log-ins that are not shared among the entire family. These may be banking accounts or accounts for which you make online payments such as your mortgage, as well as accounts with online retailers such as Amazon and iTunes. If you have to transfer funds in order to make payments and your bank hasn't reopened since the crisis and you don't have the log-in and password to do online banking, you have a financial problem on your hands. Let's say the bank is closed and you are unable to use your home computer and are working from one at the library, hospital, police station, or evacuation site. Without the user name and password to an account you need to view, you are locked out and out of luck. So gather your family around the kitchen table and make a record of all the online accounts and the user names and passwords that go with them. You'll want to revisit this list in case a password was changed.

ACCOUNT/WEBSITE ACCESS INFORMATION

Store this information in a secure location!

ACCOUNT/ WEBSITE NAME	WEBSITE ADDRESS	USER NAME	PASSWORD

TAB #7: CASH

A power outage might shut down ATM machines as well as the online Point of Sale (POS) terminals in stores that you use to pay by credit or debit card, and if that happens your community may need to revert to a cash-only commerce until the utilities are up and running again. I recommend having $100 in small bills—fives and ones—if you can, as well as a roll each of quarters, dimes, nickels, and pennies. Put the money in one of the zippered plastic pouches that attaches to the rings in your binder.

TAB #8: TITLES

Many families have collected some significant assets, such as multiple cars, boats, RVs, ATVs, airplanes, or other items where ownership is identified by a title, usually issued by your state. It may not be prudent to put the originals in the binder, but having a copy could certainly help establish your ownership if the originals were stolen, damaged, or destroyed.

TAB #9: WILLS AND TRUSTS

Depending on the size of your family and your family's circumstances, a will and the papers for a trust may be fairly lengthy. Consider keeping the originals in a safety deposit box at the bank and make copies of the most significant pieces of the will and trust and put them behind this tab in your binder. You never know what level of devastation might be dealt to your home or community by a crisis. Having the key pieces of your will or the trust you've drawn up makes the conversations with family, attorneys, the courts, or other agencies much easier. Talk with your legal advisor to find out which parts of these documents you should include in your binder, and verify that the firm has copies and has taken measures to protect them in the event of a disaster. This may also be a good time for you to evaluate these documents for any information that needs to be added, deleted, or altered. As a matter of course, you should review your will every 1 to 5 years depending on the changes to your family or assets.

TAB #10: STUFF YOU LOVE

Now that your binder is chock-full of all sorts of documents, forms, cash, and other interesting stuff, here are a couple of things I want you to think about. Do you have some special possessions that based on financial or sentimental value you just can't part with? For example, a coin or stamp collection, family photos, special awards or trophies, family heirlooms, or jewelry? You may be able to put a few of these treasures in a plastic zippered pouch that you can attach to the rings inside your binder, but probably many of these items won't even remotely fit, and you likely won't be able to collect them in your get-out-of-here evacuation. Do you have a plan to protect them from theft, fire, flood, or other disaster? If you have several heirlooms and meaningful pieces, you may want to consider a fireproof filing cabinet or safe. These aren't cheap and won't protect your valuables under all circumstances, but they are worth investigating.

TAB #11: PERSONAL BELONGINGS INVENTORY

Companies that provide home owners' insurance have suggested for years that we all take the time to make an inventory of the personal belongings we hope would be covered if our house were somehow destroyed. It's an excellent suggestion. Go through your house room by room and make a list of your furniture, jewelry, electronics, gadgets, anything of value to you. Include a description by shape, size, color, and/or configuration, such as 10-foot (3 M) black leather sectional. Make a note of the serial numbers on your electronics such as your computer, laptop, camera, TV, or video camera. To support your inventory, take photos as you go and store everything in both your binder and on your flash drive.

At this point, your binder is bursting with information that's critical to life as we know it. Crisis or not, you'll be happy to have all of these documents organized and in one place for quick and easy access. Be sure to review the contents and make updates at least every six months, and because your emergency binder contains some confidential documents, put it away in a location that's secure yet easily accessible so when disaster strikes, you can grab your binder and go.

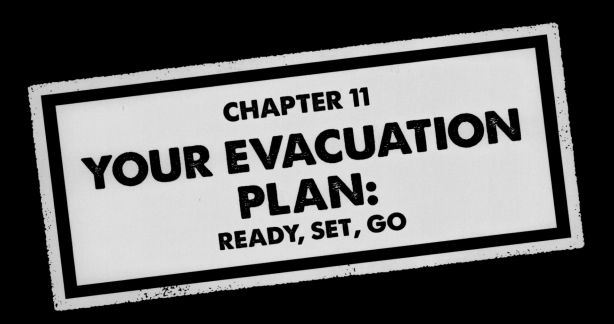

CHAPTER 11
YOUR EVACUATION PLAN:
READY, SET, GO

Emergency alert! A tornado swirls ferociously, gathering speed and strength as it careens toward your community. Authorities warn families—evacuate now! You have your 72-hour kits in the closet, your emergency binder is ready to grab out of your desk drawer, but where will you go? How will you get there? Is there gas in your car? Your safety, maybe even your survival, depends on having an exit strategy.

In this chapter, you'll learn just what to do to get ready for an evacuation. I'll help you decide where you should go, who you need to contact, and how to handle complications. You'll also learn how to make sure your car is ready to go, and even how to put together an emergency toilet in case you're stranded on the highway with no privacy. This is your final step for getting your family prepared for any emergency or disaster situation. After you work through it, your family will be calm, confident, and ready for anything life throws your way.

A tornado, hurricane, wildfire, flood, chemical leak, pandemic, terrorism, an oil spillage from a train derailment—so many possible situations could prompt local officials to urge everyone in your community to evacuate. You may hear emergency sirens blaring outside or the Emergency Broadcasting System beeping on your television or a radio message alerting you to an impending crisis. You hope it never happens, but it might without advance notice and at the most inopportune times. We tend to picture emergency situations occurring when your family is gathered at home, but that might not be the case. You might be at church. You or your spouse or both of you might be at work while your children are at school or soccer practice or at a movie. You need to have a plan for gathering everyone together on your evacuation route to safety.

You know how to store water and food and supplies in the event that you'll be stranded at home without power or water or both. You know how to put together a 72-hour kit with the items you need for the first few days after an evacuation and how to prepare a binder with all of your life-essential documents and information to take with you. Now you need to be prepared for action.

SHOULD I STAY OR SHOULD I GO?

One of the critical decisions you need to make is whether you should stay in your home and follow guidelines for sheltering in place, or do you leave the comfort and usual safety of your home. Of course this decision is based on a number of factors, such as the condition of your home or immediate neighborhood, the degree of personal preparedness for your family, and the physical condition of family members. If you are forced to leave your home because it is unsafe to stay, or local authorities are requiring all families in your area to evacuate, you really don't have a choice. If you feel you'd rather stay put because you have planned ahead and have the resources in place to care for your family, then good for you, you've done what this book suggests we all try to do.

To help with the "stay or go" decision, learn ahead of time what resources may be available to you from other groups or government agencies when a crisis occurs. One of the best organizations to look to for information is the American Red Cross (redcross.org). We've all heard of them, but we might not understand all they do to help train us for emergencies and provide disaster relief services here in the United States and throughout the world. I suggest you visit their website and poke around for the links that interest you and which may contain the most useful information. You can call them if you have specific questions (1-800-733-2767) or write to them at:

American Red Cross National Headquarters
2025 E Street, NW
Washington, DC 20006

Note that the American Red Cross has chapters and donation centers located throughout the country, and more than likely there is one reasonably close to you. If you click on the "Contact Us" link on the website you'll see a link entitled "local Red Cross chapter" where you'll find a listing of the chapters organized by state. Your local chapter can tell you where you would likely go if you needed to evacuate your home. And who knows, you may want to sign up as a volunteer. What better way to learn about the Red Cross and their resources and support your own personal preparedness plan?

Also, take some time to contact your local city and/or county government agency for guidance regarding when, how, and where you would evacuate in a crisis. I checked here in southern Utah and found that my county has an Emergency Services Department with a goal of "establishing community readiness through public education, risk assessment, planning, exercises, and interagency cooperation." I also discovered that Washington City, where we live, has a Public Safety Department whose mission is very similar. You'll find agencies like these in your area, too. Don't be afraid to call and find out how best to use their resources to benefit you and your immediate neighborhood.

YOUR EVACUATION ACTION PLAN

You won't make the decision to evacuate or not until disaster is impending, but don't wait until then to prepare for evacuation. Begin now with these steps.

1. **Make a contact card for everyone in the family that includes his or her name, address, phone numbers (cell and landline), and a list of other family members and their contact information.** If you are not together when disaster strikes, you will have each other's phone numbers and can communicate about where, how, and when to meet. Also, emergency workers or anyone who is taking care of your young children will know how to contact you or other family members. Consider including the phone number of a friend or relative who lives out of town and could serve as a central point of communication if local phone services go down. Everyone should carry his or her card at all times because you don't always have a warning about an impending disaster. Tornadoes seem to spring up out of nowhere. Earthquakes and landslides are unpredictable, and flash floods are called flash floods for a reason. Laminate your emergency contact cards, so they'll last longer, and be sure to update them as information changes.

2. **Make sure all family members have an emergency contact name in their phones listed under ICE (In Case of Emergency).** All police and emergency personnel are trained to look for ICE in all cell phones in any emergency situation.

3. **Purchase some maps for your city and county and use a permanent marker to highlight the quickest and most likely routes out of town in an evacuation.** Use different colors for each of three best routes, and indicate your order of preference—#1, #2, and #3. Make a copy of the maps for everyone who drives and for each car. Consider planning a family outing to drive each of these routes before a crisis occurs so that you'll become familiar with the roads when you are clearheaded and free of stress. It's important that everyone understand why these routes have been chosen so no one will stray from the plan unless absolutely necessary. Having a compass, which I recommend for your 72-hour kit, may come in handy if the usual landmarks become destroyed and you lose your bearings.

STORE THIS ADVICE

Please be aware of families in your neighborhood who have elderly or disabled family members and may need help in an evacuation. Talk with them ahead of time to make sure they have a plan in place and whether or not you should be a part of that plan. We should work together with our neighbors as a team during a crisis.

4. **Think through the options for where you'll go.** Do you have family or friends within 100 miles with whom you could stay? Find out what local facilities—churches or schools—are designated emergency shelters by contacting your local chapter of the American Red Cross and/or a local emergency service or public safety agency. And consider your neighborhood. In Chapter 8, I talked about the value of establishing relationships with the families who live near you. Perhaps your house is destroyed in a fire or landslide, for example, but the houses a block over are untouched. You may be able to stay with a neighbor for a short time.

5. **Register for Reverse 911.** Most cities and counties have programmed alerts to be sent out through landline phones in case of an emergency. For cell phones, there is a program called Reverse 911 available in many regions of the country. You enter your cell number into the city or county emergency management service system to receive alerts in the event of a crisis in your city or county. If you move, you will need to enter your cell phone number in the emergency management service system in your new location. To register, Google your county and state followed by Reverse 911. For example: Washington County, Utah Reverse 911. Click on the first link that comes up and then follow the instructions for registering your cell phone number.

    Let's say you have two homes, register both locations in their respective county and state Reverse 911 locations. So for instance, if you have a home in Salt Lake City, Utah, you will register all of your information with Salt Lake County Reverse 911. If you also have a home in Huntington Beach, California, you will register through Orange County Reverse 911. You can register in several counties or states depending on your situation and particular need to know, and you can delete or change the information at any time.

6. **Discuss several evacuation scenarios with your family at least once a month, so that everyone knows the plan and what to do.** Be sure to review what you would do if you were all in separate locations—work, school, shopping, whatever—and an evacuation is called. Let's assume mom is driving one daughter to music lessons, the youngest daughter is at grandma's house, dad is at work, and your son is at basketball practice. You need to determine who will pick up the bug-out bags and where you will all meet so that you can leave town together.

7. **Review communication when you're not together.** If everyone calls mom at the same time, not everyone will get through. Or the cell phone lines might be overloaded and your kids may not be able to make a call. In either case, panic might set in. Review these scenarios and come up with a plan. Suggest that family members try texting, which may go through when phone calls fail. Decide on a course of action if you cannot reach each other by phone or text. Then take it to the next level and role-play that situation. Making a plan and running through a drill before disaster occurs will help everyone respond more calmly and more effectively during a crisis.

8. **Prepare an Every Day Carry (EDC) Bag for everyone in your family.** These are small backpacks or messenger bags, you can use to carry items that would be useful in an emergency (see page 149 for more information about EDCs). Adults might pack a pair of socks and comfortable walking shoes, water, granola bars, a flashlight, extra cash, a multiuse knife, and the laminated emergency contact card. For your kids, put the contact card along with a small flashlight, snacks, water, and a small blanket into the backpack they take to school. A few items can help everyone get by until you can get together.

9. **Identify two emergency meeting locations.** One would be your home, but if disaster has struck your house or neighborhood that won't be an option. Determine a second location outside your neighborhood that everyone in your family is familiar with and could get to by car or public transportation. Keep in mind that public transportation may be shut down, depending on the crisis, and a family member may have no choice but to stay where he or she is. This is when you pull out your emergency contact cards and call each other to let everyone know where each other is and discuss how and when you will meet up.

10. **In your evacuation plans you need to account for those in your family who may be older or have disabilities.** These folks have challenges many of us don't usually think about, such as getting from Point A to Point B, hearing instructions, reading warning signs, seeing the safe path to take, or being able to quickly think on their feet. If an elderly or disabled person lives with you, be sure to include on your emergency grab-and-go list any special equipment he or she might need such as a cane, walker, or wheelchair. If this family member lives alone, arrange for someone or a group of people to look out for him or her in an emergency—a close neighbor or church member perhaps. And give that person a key to the house and any special instructions in case of an evacuation.

11. **Make a list of the items you must take with you when you leave your home, starting with the 72-hour kits and water for your whole family and your pets.** You might be thinking, *of course, I'll remember my bug-out bag,* but many people don't. I know because I've asked people how they responded and what they did in a disaster. In addition to the 72-hour kits and water, you'll want to add your emergency binder, prescription medications, and any medical devices—a nebulizer or CPAP machine, for example—to the list. Make a copy of this list and include it in your emergency bedside pouch (see page 145) along with your keys and flashlight, or if you don't have one of these, tape the list to your door.

12. **Make another list of any special heirlooms or mementos that you want to take with you.** I suggest you have a family meeting and talk about the items that are important to each person. Make a copy of this list to put in your bedside emergency pouch or tape on your door alongside your essentials list. Depending on how fast you need to leave, you may only have time to gather the essentials.

13. **Don't forget Fido.** If you are like my typical reader, you have one or more pets in your home: cats, dogs, birds, lizards, guinea pigs, hamsters, or other special little creatures. Each of these pets comes with a different set of challenges if you need to evacuate. You will need to figure out how to transport them and how to keep them warm or cool depending on the weather. Hopefully you have put together a 72-hour kit for each pet (see Chapter 9). You'll also need to try to find out ahead of time if the evacuation location you will head to—whether that's the home of friends or family or a designated shelter—will accept your pets. Red Cross sites only allow guide dogs. You might want to take a tent along in case you and your pet or pets need to sleep outside. Remember, too, that pets, like children, get upset when there's a significant disruption of their environment and routine. They may become fearful or agitated, so be sure to put small pets in a secure carrier. Have a leash or harness for your dog and consider bringing his or her crate along.

14. **If you have kids, understand that there will be added challenges.** Not only do children require their own bug-out bags, they are likely to be more upset and, therefore, temperamental during an evacuation and time away from home. This places extra demands on your parenting skills and leadership, but your kids rely on you for guidance during difficult times. Be sensitive to their fears and special needs. Let your spouse or older children share in the caregiving so you don't get burned out. This is a time for clear thinking and mature decision making. As parents, you will be the ones to make sure plans are carried out as best as possible. This will be the time when all those family conversations and practice drills will prove worthwhile.

15. **Become educated about the emergency procedures at your children's school.** You don't want to be in the dark when it comes to what will be expected of the kids, their teachers, and you in the event of a community-wide evacuation. I strongly suggest you approach the school administration and ask for a copy of their disaster plan. If they don't have one, which is unlikely, or if you don't agree with the plan as outlined, now is the time to take action so your children are protected, and you know what will take place if the school is evacuated. I doubt you'll get a phone call asking you to pick your child up, particularly if the evacuation is on short notice. If the children are to be bused to a remote location for parent pickup, you need to know that and understand under what circumstances you can retrieve your child. Also find out if there are provisions for parents to take their children out of school if a disaster such as a hurricane or tornado is pending. Be sure to discuss with your neighborhood friends who also have children in the school how you can support each other if one of you isn't available to pick up his or her kids.

STORE THIS ADVICE

When deciding on an emergency contact to include on your children's school forms, think of someone who lives close to the school and who would be able to walk and pick up your child in the event that roads were closed and you or someone living farther out were unable to get there.

16. **Make sure emergency evacuation procedures are in place at the office.** Most companies have plans identifying how different departments across the organization are to exit the building and where they are to go. Volunteers are given the responsibility over a designated area to make sure everyone exits the building. And random drills are held to practice evacuation. If your organization doesn't have a plan in place, talk with management and suggest ways that you and interested colleagues might develop and implement an emergency-preparedness plan.

17. **Make sure your car is ready to roll.** Keep the gas tank half filled at all times. You don't want to be behind hundreds of cars lined up at the gas station to fill your tank on your way out of town. Also, maintain your car regularly with oil changes, tire and battery checks, and fluid level checks. It's a good idea to have the following supplies in your car:

- ☐ Orange emergency cone(s)
- ☐ Tool kit
- ☐ Battery jumper cables
- ☐ First-aid kit
- ☐ Flashlight (preferably one that you can charge with a hand crank, in your car, or solar panels)
- ☐ Duct tape
- ☐ Bungee cords
- ☐ Compass
- ☐ Blankets
- ☐ Flares
- ☐ Cash—$100 in fives and ones plus a roll each of quarters, dimes, nickels, and pennies in case the ATM's are not working

- ☐ Fire extinguisher
- ☐ Rags
- ☐ Tow rope
- ☐ Tire gauge
- ☐ Knife, Swiss Army, or Leatherman multiuse knife
- ☐ Hand sanitizer
- ☐ Wet wipes
- ☐ Matches
- ☐ Water
- ☐ Automotive oil
- ☐ Radio, a high-quality hand-crank or battery-powered, plus extra batteries
- ☐ Emergency car toilet (see page 174)

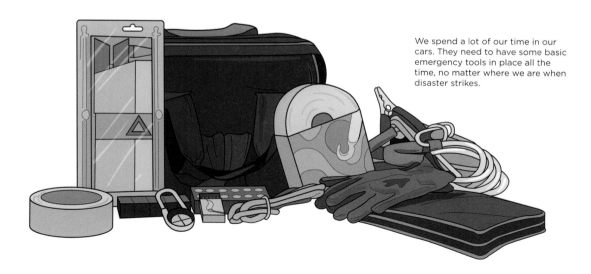

We spend a lot of our time in our cars. They need to have some basic emergency tools in place all the time, no matter where we are when disaster strikes.

Car? Check.

Family? Check.

Pets? Check.

72-hour kits? Check.

Water? Check.

Prescriptions? Check.

You are ready to head to safety.

HOW TO MAKE (AND USE) AN EMERGENCY CAR TOILET

Let's say you have been asked to evacuate your home and you and everyone else in the city is on the highway headed out of town. Cars are crawling. A few miles down the road, a little voice peeps up from the backseat, "Mommy, I have to go to the bathroom." Here's a portable potty to take with you for just such emergencies.

WHAT YOU'LL NEED

- ☐ A large coffee can or #10 can with a lid
- ☐ A roll of duct tape
- ☐ 4 (1-gallon [3.8-L]) bags
- ☐ Toilet paper
- ☐ Wet wipes
- ☐ Hand sanitizer

Your car may become your mobile bathroom using one of these handy car toilets.

HOW IT WORKS

Put everything inside the can with the lid on top until you need to use it. When nature calls, open one of the bags inside the empty can and use duct tape to attach the bag to the can. It's ready to use. The #10 cans are big enough for someone to use inside the car. Clean up with toilet paper and wipes and close the lid. Use the sanitizer on your hands. When you come to an appropriate place for waste disposal, take the bag out of the can, tie a knot in it, and throw it away.

YOU ARE PREPARED

When you began reading this book, I asked you to think about several important questions:

☐ Where would you turn for drinkable water if the supply to your home were shut down or became contaminated?

☐ How long would your food last if delivery trucks couldn't get to your local markets and shelves quickly emptied?

☐ In the event of a power outage, how would you cook meals, light your house at night, stay warm without heat, or cool without air-conditioning?

☐ Are you prepared to leave your home at a moment's notice if local authorities call for an evacuation?

Those are daunting questions, but after reading this book, you can now answer each of those questions easily and thoroughly. You have all the information you need to prepare for an emergency—to store clean water, food, cooking tools, lighting, and other supplies. You know how to pack a 72-hour kit and plan for evacuation. And you have ways to engender teamwork within your family and your neighborhood, because there is strength and comfort in numbers.

Go forward with confidence and take action now to prepare for whatever crisis may arrive at your doorstep. Whether it's a hurricane, ice storm, tornado, snowstorm, chemical spill, fire, flood, whatever the disaster... you are ready!

APPENDIX

EMERGENCY STORAGE CHECKLISTS

As you begin to gather and store water, food, and other supplies in case of a disaster, natural or other, it will be enormously helpful to have a checklist. I've created basic lists of what you need to store for three days, a week, or a month whether you are a couple or a family of 3, 4, or 5. You will want to customize them for your specific needs and wants. For example, if you have babies or toddlers, you'll want to add diapers and children's-strength over-the-counter medications to this list. If you have pets, you'll want to include food and water for them.

Also, the food list below is for a simple plan based on canned foods and commonly used packaged foods; you may choose to store freeze-dried or dehydrated foods or some combination (see Chapter 2). If you choose to diversify your food storage plans from the can-plan checklist, you may find food storage charts helpful in tracking the foods you have in storage and determining how much you need to add. You can find the charts on my blog at the following link: foodstoragemoms.com/food-storage/what-do-i-have

These checklists represent a complete and solid plan for emergency preparedness. You can use them as they are or alter them to your personal needs and desires.

FOR A COUPLE
For 3 days

WATER
- ☐ 24 gallons (91 L) of water
- ☐ 7 WaterBricks
- ☐ 3 ½ teaspoons (17 ml) Water Preserver (buy 1 bottle)

FOOD
- ☐ Protein: 6 cans of tuna, chicken, spam, roast beef, or beans
- ☐ Vegetable: 6 cans of green beans, corn, carrots, peas, or other veggies
- ☐ Fruit: 6 cans of applesauce, mandarin oranges, pineapple, or other fruit
- ☐ Grains: 1 (32-ounce [907-g]) package of rice
- ☐ Dairy: 1 (25.6-ounce [726-g]) package instant milk
- ☐ 1 (32-ounce [907-g]) package pancake mix
- ☐ 1 box biscuit mix
- ☐ 1 box cereal
- ☐ 1 (16-ounce [454-g]) jar peanut butter
- ☐ 1 (10-ounce [283-g]) jar jam
- ☐ 1 (16-ounce [454-g]) box crackers
- ☐ 1 (16-ounce [454-g]) jar salsa (adds flavor to beans, rice, meats)

COOKING SUPPLIES
- ☐ 1 butane stove
- ☐ 1 butane canister
- ☐ 2 or 3 manual can openers

LIGHTING
- ☐ 2 flashlights (consider the Goal Zero Torch 250)
- ☐ 2 indoor lanterns (consider Goal Zero Lighthouse 250)
- ☐ Extra batteries for flashlights and/or lanterns if needed

FIRST AID
- ☐ 2 first-aid kits, one for your car and one for your home (you can purchase these from the American Red Cross or make them yourself; see Chapter 5)

TEMPERATURE MANAGEMENT
For warmth in the cold
- ☐ 4 to 6 blankets
- ☐ 2 woolen hats
- ☐ 2 pairs of gloves
- ☐ 2 pairs of mittens
- ☐ 2 scarves
- ☐ 2 winter jackets or coats

To cool your body in the heat
- ☐ 2 squirt bottles
- ☐ 2 cooling towels

PERSONAL HYGIENE
- ☐ 2 toothbrushes (plus extras for guests)
- ☐ 1 (6-ounce [170-g]) tube of toothpaste
- ☐ 1 container of dental floss
- ☐ 1 (8-ounce [237-ml]) bottle of shampoo
- ☐ 1 box of wet wipes (100 per container)
- ☐ 1 (8-ounce [237-ml]) bottle of hand sanitizer

- ☐ 1 bar of soap
- ☐ 1 (8-ounce [237-ml]) tube or bottle of hand moisturizer
- ☐ 1 (8-ounce [237-ml]) bottle of body lotion
- ☐ Feminine products if needed

PAPER DISHES
- ☐ 6 of each: paper plates, bowls, and cups
- ☐ 6 of each: plastic forks, knives, and spoons
- ☐ 6 paper napkins
- ☐ 1 roll of paper towels

CLEANING SUPPLIES
- ☐ 1 box of wet wipes (100 count)
- ☐ 1 (20-ounce [591-ml]) bottle of unscented bleach

MISCELLANEOUS
- ☐ 1 multipurpose knife, such as Swiss Army or Leatherman
- ☐ 1 box 300-count wooden matches
- ☐ 1 roll of duct tape (9 mm–2 inches [5 cm] by 60 yards [55 M])

For 7 days

WATER
- ☐ 56 gallons (212 L) of water
- ☐ 16 WaterBricks
- ☐ 8 teaspoons (40 ml) Water Preserver (buy 2 bottles)

FOOD
- ☐ Protein: 14 cans of tuna, chicken, spam, roast beef, or beans
- ☐ Vegetable: 14 cans of green beans, corn, carrots, peas, or other veggies
- ☐ Fruit: 14 cans of applesauce, mandarin oranges, pineapple, or other fruit
- ☐ Grains: 1 (32-ounce [907-g]) package of rice
- ☐ Dairy: 2 (25.6-ounce [726-g]) packages instant milk
- ☐ 1 (32-ounce [907-g]) package pancake mix
- ☐ 1 box biscuit mix
- ☐ 1 box cereal
- ☐ 1 (16-ounce [454-g]) jar peanut butter
- ☐ 1 (10-ounce [283-g]) jar jam
- ☐ 1 (16-ounce [454-g]) box crackers
- ☐ 1 (16-ounce [454-g]) jar salsa (adds flavor to beans, rice, meats)

COOKING SUPPLIES
- ☐ 1 butane stove
- ☐ 1 butane canisters
- ☐ 2 or 3 manual can openers

LIGHTING
- ☐ 2 flashlights (consider the Goal Zero Torch 250)
- ☐ 2 indoor lanterns (consider Goal Zero Lighthouse 250)
- ☐ Extra batteries for flashlights and/or lanterns if needed
- ☐ First Aid
- ☐ 2 first-aid kits, one for your car and one for your home (you can purchase these from the American Red Cross or make them yourself; see Chapter 5)

TEMPERATURE MANAGEMENT
For warmth in the cold:
- ☐ 4 to 6 blankets
- ☐ 2 woolen hats
- ☐ 2 pairs of gloves
- ☐ 2 pairs of mittens
- ☐ 2 scarves
- ☐ 2 winter jackets or coats
To cool your body in the heat
- ☐ 2 squirt bottles
- ☐ 2 cooling towels

PERSONAL HYGIENE
- ☐ 2 toothbrushes (plus extras for guests)
- ☐ 1 (6-ounce [170-g]) tube of toothpaste
- ☐ 1 container of dental floss
- ☐ 1 (8-ounce [237-ml]) bottle of shampoo
- ☐ 1 box of wet wipes (100 per container)
- ☐ 2 (8-ounce [237-ml]) bottles of hand sanitizer
- ☐ 1 bar of soap
- ☐ 1 (8-ounce [237-ml]) tube or bottle of hand moisturizer
- ☐ 1 (8-ounce [237-ml]) bottle of body lotion
- ☐ Feminine products if needed

PAPER DISHES
- ☐ 14 of each: paper plates, bowls, and cups
- ☐ 14 of each: plastic forks, knives, and spoons
- ☐ 14 paper napkins
- ☐ 2 rolls of paper towels

CLEANING SUPPLIES
- ☐ 1 box of wet wipes (100 count)
- ☐ 1 (30-ounce [887-ml]) bottle of unscented bleach

MISCELLANEOUS
- ☐ 1 multipurpose knife, such as Swiss Army or Leatherman
- ☐ 1 box 300-count wooden matches
- ☐ 1 roll of duct tape (9 mm–2 inches [5 cm] by 60 yards [55 M])

For 1 month

WATER
- ☐ 224 gallons (848 L) of water
- ☐ 64 WaterBricks
- ☐ 32 teaspoons (160 ml) Water Preserver (buy 2 bottles)

FOOD
- ☐ Protein: 60 cans of tuna, chicken, spam, roast beef, or beans
- ☐ Vegetable: 60 cans of green beans, corn, carrots, peas, or other veggies
- ☐ Fruit: 60 cans of applesauce, mandarin oranges, pineapple, or other fruit
- ☐ Grains: 3 (32-ounce [907-g]) packages of rice
- ☐ Dairy: 5 (25.6-ounce [726-g]) packages instant milk
- ☐ 2 (32-ounce [907-g]) packages pancake mix
- ☐ 2 boxes biscuit mix
- ☐ 4 boxes cereal

(continued)

- ☐ 4 (16-ounce [454-g]) jars peanut butter
- ☐ 4 (10-ounce [283-g]) jars jam
- ☐ 4 (16-ounce [454-g]) boxes crackers
- ☐ 4 (16-ounce [454-g]) jars salsa (adds flavor to beans, rice, meats)

COOKING SUPPLIES
- ☐ 1 butane stove
- ☐ 2 butane canisters
- ☐ 2 or 3 manual can openers

LIGHTING
- ☐ 2 flashlights (consider the Goal Zero Torch 250)
- ☐ 2 indoor lanterns (consider Goal Zero Lighthouse 250)
- ☐ Extra batteries for flashlights and/or lanterns if needed

FIRST AID
- ☐ 2 first-aid kits, one for your car and one for your home (you can purchase these from the American Red Cross or make them yourself; see Chapter 5)

TEMPERATURE MANAGEMENT
For warmth in the cold
- ☐ 4 to 6 blankets
- ☐ 4 woolen hats
- ☐ 2 pairs of gloves
- ☐ 2 pairs of mittens
- ☐ 2 scarves
- ☐ 2 winter jackets or coats

To cool your body in the heat
- ☐ 2 squirt bottles
- ☐ 2 cooling towels

PERSONAL HYGIENE
- ☐ 2 toothbrushes (plus extras for guests)
- ☐ 1 (6-ounce [170-g]) tube of toothpaste
- ☐ 1 container of dental floss
- ☐ 1 (8-ounce [237-ml]) bottle of shampoo
- ☐ 2 boxes of wet wipes (100 per container)
- ☐ 4 (8-ounce [237-ml]) bottles of hand sanitizer
- ☐ 1 bar of soap
- ☐ 1 (8-ounce [237-ml]) tube or bottle of hand moisturizer
- ☐ 1 (8-ounce [237-ml]) bottle of body lotion
- ☐ Feminine products if needed

PAPER DISHES
- ☐ 60 of each: paper plates, bowls, and cups
- ☐ 60 of each: plastic forks, knives, and spoons
- ☐ 60 paper napkins
- ☐ 8 rolls of paper towels

CLEANING SUPPLIES
- ☐ 4 boxes of wet wipes (100 count)
- ☐ 1 (55-ounce [1.6-L]) bottle of unscented bleach

MISCELLANEOUS
- ☐ 1 multipurpose knife, such as Swiss Army or Leatherman
- ☐ 2 boxes 300-count wooden matches
- ☐ 2 rolls of duct tape (9 mm–2 inches [5 cm] by 60 yards [55 M])

FOR A FAMILY OF THREE
For 3 days

WATER
- ☐ 36 gallons (136 L) of water
- ☐ 11 WaterBricks
- ☐ 5 teaspoons (25 ml) Water Preserver (buy 1 bottle)

FOOD
- ☐ Protein: 9 cans of tuna, chicken, spam, roast beef, or beans
- ☐ Vegetable: 9 cans of green beans, corn, carrots, peas, or other veggies
- ☐ Fruit: 9 cans of applesauce, mandarin oranges, pineapple, or other fruit
- ☐ Grains: 1 (32-ounce [907-g]) package of rice
- ☐ Dairy: 1 (25.6-ounce [726-g]) package instant milk
- ☐ 1 (32-ounce [907-g]) package pancake mix
- ☐ 1 box biscuit mix
- ☐ 1 box cereal
- ☐ 1 (16-ounce [454-g]) jar peanut butter
- ☐ 1 (10-ounce [283-g]) jar jam
- ☐ 1 (16-ounce [454-g]) box crackers
- ☐ 1 (16-ounce [454-g]) jar salsa (adds flavor to beans, rice, meats)

COOKING SUPPLIES
- ☐ 1 butane stove
- ☐ 1 butane canister
- ☐ 2 or 3 manual can openers

LIGHTING
- ☐ 3 flashlights (consider the Goal Zero Torch 250)
- ☐ 2 indoor lanterns (consider Goal Zero Lighthouse 250)
- ☐ Extra batteries for flashlights and/or lanterns if needed

FIRST AID
- ☐ 2 first-aid kits, one for your car and one for your home (you can purchase these from the American Red Cross or make them yourself; see Chapter 5)

TEMPERATURE MANAGEMENT
For warmth in the cold
- ☐ 6 to 9 blankets
- ☐ 3 woolen hats
- ☐ 3 pairs of gloves
- ☐ 3 pairs of mittens
- ☐ 3 scarves
- ☐ 3 winter jackets or coats

To cool your body in the heat
- ☐ 3 squirt bottles
- ☐ 3 cooling towels

PERSONAL HYGIENE
- ☐ 3 toothbrushes (plus extras for guests)
- ☐ 1 (6-ounce [170-g]) tube of toothpaste
- ☐ 1 container of dental floss
- ☐ 1 (8-ounce [237-ml]) bottle of shampoo
- ☐ 1 box of wet wipes (100 per container)
- ☐ 1 (8-ounce [237-ml]) bottle of hand sanitizer

- ☐ 1 bar of soap
- ☐ 1 (8-ounce [237-ml]) tube or bottle of hand moisturizer
- ☐ 1 (8-ounce [237-ml]) bottle of body lotion
- ☐ Feminine products if needed
- ☐ 24 cloth diapers if there's a baby in the household

PAPER DISHES
- ☐ 9 of each: paper plates, bowls, and cups
- ☐ 9 of each: plastic forks, knives, and spoons
- ☐ 9 paper napkins
- ☐ 1 roll of paper towels

CLEANING SUPPLIES
- ☐ 1 box of wet wipes (100 count)
- ☐ 1 (30-ounce [887-ml]) bottle of unscented bleach

MISCELLANEOUS
- ☐ 1 multipurpose knife, such as Swiss Army or Leatherman
- ☐ 1 box 300-count wooden matches
- ☐ 1 roll of duct tape (9 mm–2 inches [5 cm] by 60 yards [55 M])

For 7 days

WATER
- ☐ 84 gallons (318 L) of water
- ☐ 24 WaterBricks
- ☐ 12 teaspoons (60 ml) Water Preserver (buy 2 bottles)

FOOD
- ☐ Protein: 21 cans of tuna, chicken, spam, roast beef, or beans
- ☐ Vegetable: 21 cans of green beans, corn, carrots, peas, or other veggies
- ☐ Fruit: 21 cans of applesauce, mandarin oranges, pineapple, or other fruit
- ☐ Grains: 1 (32-ounce [907-g]) package of rice
- ☐ Dairy: 2 (25.6-ounce [726-g]) packages instant milk
- ☐ 1 (32-ounce [907-g]) package pancake mix
- ☐ 1 box biscuit mix
- ☐ 2 boxes cereal
- ☐ 2 (16-ounce [454-g]) jars peanut butter
- ☐ 2 (10-ounce [283-g]) jars jam
- ☐ 2 (16-ounce [454-g]) boxes crackers
- ☐ 2 (16-ounce [454-g]) jars salsa (adds flavor to beans, rice, meats)

COOKING SUPPLIES
- ☐ 1 butane stove
- ☐ 1 butane canister
- ☐ 2 or 3 manual can openers

LIGHTING
- ☐ 3 flashlights (consider the Goal Zero Torch 250)
- ☐ 2 indoor lanterns (consider Goal Zero Lighthouse 250)
- ☐ Extra batteries for flashlights and/or lanterns if needed

FIRST AID
- ☐ 2 first-aid kits, one for your car and one for your home (you can purchase these from the American Red Cross or make them yourself; see Chapter 5)

TEMPERATURE MANAGEMENT
For warmth in the cold
- ☐ 6 to 9 blankets
- ☐ 3 woolen hats
- ☐ 3 pairs of gloves
- ☐ 3 pairs of mittens
- ☐ 3 scarves
- ☐ 3 winter jackets or coats

To cool your body in the heat
- ☐ 3 squirt bottles
- ☐ 3 cooling towels

PERSONAL HYGIENE
- ☐ 3 toothbrushes (plus extras for guests)
- ☐ 1 (6-ounce [170-g]) tube of toothpaste
- ☐ 1 container of dental floss
- ☐ 1 (8-ounce [237-ml]) bottle of shampoo
- ☐ 2 boxes of wet wipes (100 per container)
- ☐ 2 (8-ounce [237-ml]) bottles of hand sanitizer
- ☐ 1 bar of soap
- ☐ 1 (8-ounce [237-ml]) tube or bottle of hand moisturizer
- ☐ 1 (8-ounce [237-ml]) bottle of body lotion
- ☐ Feminine products if needed
- ☐ 24 cloth diapers if there's a baby in the household

PAPER DISHES
- ☐ 21 of each: paper plates, bowls, and cups
- ☐ 21 of each: plastic forks, knives, and spoons
- ☐ 21 paper napkins
- ☐ 2 rolls of paper towels

CLEANING SUPPLIES
- ☐ 1 box of wet wipes (100 count)
- ☐ 1 (55-ounce [1.6-L]) bottle of unscented bleach

MISCELLANEOUS
- ☐ 1 multipurpose knife, such as Swiss Army or Leatherman
- ☐ 1 box 300-count wooden matches
- ☐ 1 roll of duct tape (9 mm–2 inches [5 cm] by 60 yards [55 M])

For 1 month

WATER
- ☐ 336 gallons (1,272 L) of water
- ☐ 96 WaterBricks
- ☐ 48 teaspoons (240 ml) Water Preserver (buy 7 bottles)

FOOD
- ☐ Protein: 90 cans of tuna, chicken, spam, roast beef, or beans
- ☐ Vegetable: 90 cans of green beans, corn, carrots, peas, or other veggies
- ☐ Fruit: 90 cans of applesauce, mandarin oranges, pineapple, or other fruit
- ☐ Grains: 5 (32-ounce [907-g]) packages of rice
- ☐ Dairy: 9 (25.6-ounce [726-g]) packages instant milk

(continued)

- ☐ 3 (32-ounce [907-g]) packages pancake mix
- ☐ 2 boxes biscuit mix
- ☐ 6 boxes cereal
- ☐ 6 (16-ounce [454-g]) jars peanut butter
- ☐ 6 (10-ounce [283-g]) jars jam
- ☐ 4 (16-ounce [454-g]) boxes crackers
- ☐ 6 (16-ounce [454-g]) jars salsa (adds flavor to beans, rice, meats)

COOKING SUPPLIES
- ☐ 1 butane stove
- ☐ 2 butane canisters
- ☐ 2 or 3 manual can openers

LIGHTING
- ☐ 3 flashlights (consider the Goal Zero Torch 250)
- ☐ 2 indoor lanterns (consider Goal Zero Lighthouse 250)
- ☐ Extra batteries for flashlights and/or lanterns if needed

FIRST AID
- ☐ 2 first-aid kits, one for your car and one for your home (you can purchase these from the American Red Cross or make them yourself; see Chapter 5)

TEMPERATURE MANAGEMENT
For warmth in the cold
- ☐ 6 to 9 blankets
- ☐ 6 woolen hats
- ☐ 3 pairs of gloves
- ☐ 3 pairs of mittens
- ☐ 3 scarves
- ☐ 3 winter jackets or coats

To cool your body in the heat
- ☐ 3 squirt bottles
- ☐ 3 cooling towels

PERSONAL HYGIENE
- ☐ 3 toothbrushes (plus extras for guests)
- ☐ 2 (6-ounce [170-g]) tubes of toothpaste
- ☐ 2 containers of dental floss
- ☐ 1 (8-ounce [237-ml]) bottle of shampoo
- ☐ 8 boxes of wet wipes (100 per container)
- ☐ 8 (8-ounce [237-ml]) bottles of hand sanitizer
- ☐ 2 bars of soap
- ☐ 2 (8-ounce [237-ml]) tubes or bottles of hand moisturizer
- ☐ 2 (8-ounce [237-ml]) bottles of body lotion
- ☐ Feminine products if needed
- ☐ 24 cloth diapers if there's a baby in the household

PAPER DISHES
- ☐ 90 of each: paper plates, bowls, and cups
- ☐ 90 of each: plastic forks, knives, and spoons
- ☐ 90 paper napkins
- ☐ 8 rolls of paper towels

CLEANING SUPPLIES
- ☐ 4 boxes of wet wipes (100 count)
- ☐ 1 (55-ounce [1.6-L]) bottle of unscented bleach

MISCELLANEOUS
- ☐ 1 multipurpose knife, such as Swiss Army or Leatherman
- ☐ 2 boxes 300-count wooden matches
- ☐ 2 rolls of duct tape (9 mm–2 inches [5 cm] by 60 yards [55 M])

FOR A FAMILY OF FOUR
For 3 days

WATER
- ☐ 48 gallons (182 L) of water
- ☐ 14 WaterBricks
- ☐ 5 teaspoons (25 ml) Water Preserver (buy 1 bottle)

FOOD
- ☐ Protein: 12 cans of tuna, chicken, spam, roast beef, or beans
- ☐ Vegetable: 12 cans of green beans, corn, carrots, peas, or other veggies
- ☐ Fruit: 12 cans of applesauce, mandarin oranges, pineapple, or other fruit
- ☐ Grains: 1 (32-ounce [907-g]) package of rice
- ☐ Dairy: 1 (25.6-ounce [726-g]) package instant milk
- ☐ 1 (32-ounce [907-g]) package pancake mix
- ☐ 1 box biscuit mix
- ☐ 1 box cereal
- ☐ 1 (16-ounce [454-g]) jar peanut butter
- ☐ 1 (10-ounce [283-g]) jar jam
- ☐ 1 (16-ounce [454-g]) box crackers
- ☐ 1 (16-ounce [454-g]) jar salsa (adds flavor to beans, rice, meats)

COOKING SUPPLIES
- ☐ 1 butane stove
- ☐ 2 butane canisters
- ☐ 2 or 3 manual can openers

LIGHTING
- ☐ 4 flashlights (consider the Goal Zero Torch 250)
- ☐ 2 indoor lanterns (consider Goal Zero Lighthouse 250)
- ☐ Extra batteries for flashlights and/or lanterns if needed

FIRST AID
- ☐ 2 first-aid kits, one for your car and one for your home (you can purchase these from the American Red Cross or make them yourself; see Chapter 5)

TEMPERATURE MANAGEMENT
For warmth in the cold
- ☐ 8 to 12 blankets
- ☐ 4 woolen hats
- ☐ 4 pairs of gloves
- ☐ 4 pairs of mittens
- ☐ 4 scarves
- ☐ 4 winter jackets or coats

To cool your body in the heat
- ☐ 4 squirt bottles
- ☐ 4 cooling towels

PERSONAL HYGIENE
- ☐ 4 toothbrushes (plus extras for guests)
- ☐ 1 (6-ounce [170-g]) tube of toothpaste
- ☐ 1 container of dental floss
- ☐ 1 (8-ounce [237-ml]) bottle of shampoo
- ☐ 2 boxes of wet wipes (100 per container)
- ☐ 2 (8-ounce [237-ml]) bottles of hand sanitizer
- ☐ 1 bar of soap
- ☐ 1 (8-ounce [237-ml]) tube or bottle of hand moisturizer
- ☐ 1 (8-ounce [237-ml]) bottle of body lotion
- ☐ Feminine products if needed
- ☐ 24 cloth diapers if there's a baby in the household

PAPER DISHES
- ☐ 12 of each: paper plates, bowls, and cups
- ☐ 12 of each: plastic forks, knives, and spoons
- ☐ 12 paper napkins
- ☐ 2 rolls of paper towels

CLEANING SUPPLIES
- ☐ 1 box of wet wipes (100 count)
- ☐ 1 (55-ounce [1.6-L]) bottle of unscented bleach

MISCELLANEOUS
- ☐ 1 multipurpose knife, such as Swiss Army or Leatherman
- ☐ 1 box 300-count wooden matches
- ☐ 1 roll of duct tape (9 mm–2 inches [5 cm] by 60 yards [55 M])

For 7 days
WATER
- ☐ 112 gallons (424 L) of water
- ☐ 32 WaterBricks
- ☐ 16 teaspoons (80 ml) Water Preserver (buy 3 bottles)

FOOD
- ☐ Protein: 28 cans of tuna, chicken, spam, roast beef, or beans
- ☐ Vegetable: 28 cans of green beans, corn, carrots, peas, or other veggies
- ☐ Fruit: 28 cans of applesauce, mandarin oranges, pineapple, or other fruit
- ☐ Grains: 2 (32-ounce [907-g]) packages of rice
- ☐ Dairy: 3 (25.6-ounce [726-g]) packages instant milk
- ☐ 1 (32-ounce [907-g]) package pancake mix
- ☐ 1 box biscuit mix
- ☐ 2 boxes cereal
- ☐ 2 (16-ounce [454-g]) jars peanut butter
- ☐ 2 (10-ounce [283-g]) jars jam
- ☐ 2 (16-ounce [454-g]) boxes crackers
- ☐ 2 (16-ounce [454-g]) jars salsa (adds flavor to beans, rice, meats)

COOKING SUPPLIES
- ☐ 1 butane stove
- ☐ 1 butane canister
- ☐ 2 or 3 manual can openers

LIGHTING
- ☐ 4 flashlights (consider the Goal Zero Torch 250)
- ☐ 2 indoor lanterns (consider Goal Zero Lighthouse 250)
- ☐ Extra batteries for flashlights and/or lanterns if needed

FIRST AID
- ☐ 2 first-aid kits, one for your car and one for your home (you can purchase these from the American Red Cross or make them yourself; see Chapter 5)

TEMPERATURE MANAGEMENT
For warmth in the cold
- ☐ 8 to 12 blankets
- ☐ 4 woolen hats
- ☐ 4 pairs of gloves
- ☐ 4 pairs of mittens
- ☐ 4 scarves
- ☐ 4 winter jackets or coats

To cool your body in the heat
- ☐ 4 squirt bottles
- ☐ 4 cooling towels

PERSONAL HYGIENE
- ☐ 4 toothbrushes (plus extras for guests)
- ☐ 1 (6-ounce [170-g]) tube of toothpaste
- ☐ 1 container of dental floss
- ☐ 1 (8-ounce [237-ml]) bottle of shampoo
- ☐ 2 boxes of wet wipes (100 per container)
- ☐ 2 (8-ounce [237-ml]) bottles of hand sanitizer
- ☐ 1 bar of soap
- ☐ 2 (8-ounce [237-ml]) tubes or bottles of hand moisturizer
- ☐ 2 (8-ounce [237-ml]) bottles of body lotion
- ☐ Feminine products if needed
- ☐ 24 cloth diapers if there's a baby in the household

PAPER DISHES
- ☐ 28 of each: paper plates, bowls, and cups
- ☐ 28 of each: plastic forks, knives, and spoons
- ☐ 28 paper napkins
- ☐ 4 rolls of paper towels

CLEANING SUPPLIES
- ☐ 1 box of wet wipes (100 count)
- ☐ 1 (55-ounce [1.6-L]) bottle of unscented bleach

MISCELLANEOUS
- ☐ 1 multipurpose knife, such as Swiss Army or Leatherman
- ☐ 1 box 300-count wooden matches
- ☐ 1 roll of duct tape (9 mm–2 inches [5 cm] by 60 yards [55 M])

For 1 month
WATER
- ☐ 448 gallons (1,696 L) of water
- ☐ 128 WaterBricks
- ☐ 64 teaspoons (320 ml) Water Preserver (buy 9 bottles)

(continued)

FOOD

- ☐ Protein: 120 cans of tuna, chicken, spam, roast beef, or beans
- ☐ Vegetable: 120 cans of green beans, corn, carrots, peas, or other veggies
- ☐ Fruit: 120 cans of applesauce, mandarin oranges, pineapple, or other fruit
- ☐ Grains: 6 (32-ounce [907-g]) packages of rice
- ☐ Dairy: 12 (25.6-ounce [726-g]) packages instant milk
- ☐ 6 (32-ounce [907-g]) packages pancake mix
- ☐ 3 boxes biscuit mix
- ☐ 6 boxes cereal
- ☐ 9 (16-ounce [454-g]) jars peanut butter
- ☐ 9 (10-ounce [283-g]) jars jam
- ☐ 5 (16-ounce [454-g]) boxes crackers
- ☐ 8 (16-ounce [454-g]) jars salsa (adds flavor to beans, rice, meats)

COOKING SUPPLIES

- ☐ 1 butane stove
- ☐ 2 butane canisters
- ☐ 2 or 3 manual can openers

LIGHTING

- ☐ 4 flashlights (consider the Goal Zero Torch 250)
- ☐ 2 indoor lanterns (consider Goal Zero Lighthouse 250)
- ☐ Extra batteries for flashlights and/or lanterns if needed

FIRST AID

- ☐ 2 first-aid kits, one for your car and one for your home (you can purchase these from the American Red Cross or make them yourself; see Chapter 5)

TEMPERATURE MANAGEMENT

For warmth in the cold

- ☐ 8 to 12 blankets
- ☐ 8 woolen hats
- ☐ 4 pairs of gloves
- ☐ 4 pairs of mittens
- ☐ 4 scarves
- ☐ 4 winter jackets or coats

To cool your body in the heat

- ☐ 4 squirt bottles
- ☐ 4 cooling towels

PERSONAL HYGIENE

- ☐ 4 toothbrushes (plus extras for guests)
- ☐ 2 (6-ounce [170-g]) tubes of toothpaste
- ☐ 2 containers of dental floss
- ☐ 2 (8-ounce [237-ml]) bottles of shampoo
- ☐ 3 boxes of wet wipes (100 per container)
- ☐ 8 (8-ounce [237-ml]) bottles of hand sanitizer
- ☐ 1 bar of soap
- ☐ 2 (8-ounce [237-ml]) tubes or bottles of hand moisturizer
- ☐ 2 (8-ounce [237-ml]) bottles of body lotion
- ☐ Feminine products if needed
- ☐ 24 cloth diapers if there's a baby in the household

PAPER DISHES

- ☐ 120 of each: paper plates, bowls, and cups
- ☐ 120 of each: plastic forks, knives, and spoons
- ☐ 120 paper napkins
- ☐ 16 rolls of paper towels

CLEANING SUPPLIES

- ☐ 4 boxes of wet wipes (100 count)
- ☐ 1 gallon (3.8 L) of unscented bleach

MISCELLANEOUS

- ☐ 1 multipurpose knife, such as Swiss Army or Leatherman
- ☐ 2 boxes 300-count wooden matches
- ☐ 2 rolls of duct tape (9 mm–2 inches [5 cm] by 60 yards [55 M])

FOR A FAMILY OF FIVE

For 3 days

WATER

- ☐ 60 gallons (227 L) of water
- ☐ 18 Water Bricks
- ☐ 8 ½ teaspoons (43 ml) Water Preserver (buy 2 bottles)

FOOD

- ☐ Protein: 15 cans of tuna, chicken, spam, roast beef, or beans
- ☐ Vegetable: 15 cans of green beans, corn, carrots, peas, or other veggies
- ☐ Fruit: 15 cans of applesauce, mandarin oranges, pineapple, or other fruit
- ☐ Grains: 1 (32-ounce [907-g]) package of rice
- ☐ Dairy: 2 (25.6-ounce [726-g]) packages instant milk
- ☐ 1 (32-ounce [907-g]) package pancake mix
- ☐ 1 box biscuit mix
- ☐ 1 box cereal
- ☐ 1 (16-ounce [454-g]) jar peanut butter
- ☐ 1 (10-ounce [283-g]) jar jam
- ☐ 1 (16-ounce [454-g]) box crackers
- ☐ 1 (16-ounce [454-g]) jar salsa (adds flavor to beans, rice, meats)

COOKING SUPPLIES

- ☐ 1 butane stove
- ☐ 1 butane canister
- ☐ 2 or 3 manual can openers

LIGHTING

- ☐ 5 flashlights (consider the Goal Zero Torch 250)
- ☐ 2 indoor lanterns (consider Goal Zero Lighthouse 250)
- ☐ Extra batteries for flashlights and/or lanterns if needed

FIRST AID

- ☐ 2 first-aid kits, one for your car and one for your home (you can purchase these from the American Red Cross or make them yourself; see Chapter 5)

TEMPERATURE MANAGEMENT

For warmth in the cold

- ☐ 10 to 15 blankets
- ☐ 5 woolen hats
- ☐ 5 pairs of gloves
- ☐ 5 pairs of mittens
- ☐ 5 scarves
- ☐ 5 winter jackets or coats

To cool your body in the heat

- ☐ 5 squirt bottles
- ☐ 5 cooling towels

PERSONAL HYGIENE

- ☐ 5 toothbrushes (plus extras for guests)
- ☐ 1 (6-ounce [170-g]) tube of toothpaste
- ☐ 1 container of dental floss
- ☐ 1 (8-ounce [237-ml]) bottle of shampoo
- ☐ 1 box of wet wipes (100 per container)
- ☐ 2 (8-ounce [237-ml]) bottles of hand sanitizer
- ☐ 1 bar of soap
- ☐ 2 (8-ounce [237-ml]) tubes or bottles of hand moisturizer
- ☐ 2 (8-ounce [237-ml]) bottles of body lotion
- ☐ Feminine products if needed
- ☐ 24 cloth diapers if there's a baby in the household

PAPER DISHES

- ☐ 15 of each: paper plates, bowls, and cups
- ☐ 15 of each: plastic forks, knives, and spoons
- ☐ 15 paper napkins
- ☐ 2 rolls of paper towels

CLEANING SUPPLIES

- ☐ 1 box of wet wipes (100 count)
- ☐ 1 (55-ounce [1.6-L]) bottle of unscented bleach

MISCELLANEOUS

- ☐ 1 multipurpose knife, such as Swiss Army or Leatherman
- ☐ 1 box 300-count wooden matches
- ☐ 1 roll of duct tape (9 mm–2 inches [5 cm] by 60 yards [55 M])

For 7 days

WATER

- ☐ 140 gallons (530 L) of water
- ☐ 40 WaterBricks
- ☐ 20 teaspoons (100 ml) Water Preserver (buy 3 bottles)

FOOD

- ☐ Protein: 35 cans of tuna, chicken, spam, roast beef, or beans
- ☐ Vegetable: 35 cans of green beans, corn, carrots, peas, or other veggies
- ☐ Fruit: 35 cans of applesauce, mandarin oranges, pineapple, or other fruit
- ☐ Grains: 2 (32-ounce [907-g]) packages of rice
- ☐ Dairy: 7 (25.6-ounce [726-g]) packages instant milk
- ☐ 2 (32-ounce [907-g]) packages pancake mix
- ☐ 2 boxes biscuit mix

- ☐ 3 boxes cereal
- ☐ 2 (16-ounce [454-g]) jars peanut butter
- ☐ 2 (10-ounce [283-g]) jars jam
- ☐ 2 (16-ounce [454-g]) boxes crackers
- ☐ 2 (16-ounce [454-g]) jars salsa (adds flavor to beans, rice, meats)

COOKING SUPPLIES

- ☐ 1 butane stove
- ☐ 1 butane canisters
- ☐ 2 or 3 manual can openers

LIGHTING

- ☐ 5 flashlights (consider the Goal Zero Torch 250)
- ☐ 2 indoor lanterns (consider Goal Zero Lighthouse 250)
- ☐ Extra batteries for flashlights and/or lanterns if needed

FIRST AID

- ☐ 2 first-aid kits, one for your car and one for your home (you can purchase these from the American Red Cross or make them yourself; see Chapter 5)

TEMPERATURE MANAGEMENT

For warmth in the cold

- ☐ 10 to 15 blankets
- ☐ 5 woolen hats
- ☐ 5 pairs of gloves
- ☐ 5 pairs of mittens
- ☐ 5 scarves
- ☐ 5 winter jackets or coats

To cool your body in the heat

- ☐ 5 squirt bottles
- ☐ 5 cooling towels

PERSONAL HYGIENE

- ☐ 5 toothbrushes (plus extras for guests)
- ☐ 1 (6-ounce [170-g]) tube of toothpaste
- ☐ 1 container of dental floss
- ☐ 1 (8-ounce [237-ml]) bottle of shampoo
- ☐ 3 boxes of wet wipes (100 per container)
- ☐ 3 (8-ounce [237-ml]) bottles of hand sanitizer
- ☐ 1 bar of soap
- ☐ 3 (8-ounce [237-ml]) tubes or bottles of hand moisturizer
- ☐ 3 (8-ounce [237-ml]) bottles of body lotion
- ☐ Feminine products if needed
- ☐ 24 cloth diapers if there's a baby in the household

PAPER DISHES

- ☐ 35 of each: paper plates, bowls, and cups
- ☐ 35 of each: plastic forks, knives, and spoons
- ☐ 35 paper napkins
- ☐ 4 rolls of paper towels

CLEANING SUPPLIES

- ☐ 1 box of wet wipes (100 count)
- ☐ 1 (55-ounce [1.6-L]) bottle of unscented bleach

MISCELLANEOUS

- ☐ 1 multipurpose knife, such as Swiss Army or Leatherman

(continued)

- ☐ 1 box 300-count wooden matches
- ☐ 1 roll of duct tape (9 mm–2 inches [5 cm] by 60 yards [55 M])

For 1 month

WATER
- ☐ 560 gallons (2,120 L) of water
- ☐ 160 WaterBricks
- ☐ 80 teaspoons (400 ml) Water Preserver (buy 11 bottles)

FOOD
- ☐ Protein: 150 cans of tuna, chicken, spam, roast beef, or beans
- ☐ Vegetable: 150 cans of green beans, corn, carrots, peas, or other veggies
- ☐ Fruit: 150 cans of applesauce, mandarin oranges, pineapple, or other fruit
- ☐ Grains: 8 (32-ounce [907-g]) packages of rice
- ☐ Dairy: 14 (25.6-ounce [726-g]) packages instant milk
- ☐ 8 (32-ounce [907-g]) packages pancake mix
- ☐ 4 boxes biscuit mix
- ☐ 10 boxes cereal
- ☐ 11 (16-ounce [454-g]) jars peanut butter
- ☐ 11 (10-ounce [283-g]) jars jam
- ☐ 5 (16-ounce [454-g]) boxes crackers
- ☐ 11 (16-ounce [454-g]) jars salsa (adds flavor to beans, rice, meats)

COOKING SUPPLIES
- ☐ 1 butane stove
- ☐ 2 butane canisters
- ☐ 2 or 3 manual can openers

LIGHTING
- ☐ 5 flashlights (consider the Goal Zero Torch 250)
- ☐ 2 indoor lanterns (consider Goal Zero Lighthouse 250)
- ☐ Extra batteries for flashlights and/or lanterns if needed

FIRST AID
- ☐ 2 first-aid kits, one for your car and one for your home (you can purchase these from the American Red Cross or make them yourself; see Chapter 5)

TEMPERATURE MANAGEMENT
For warmth in the cold
- ☐ 10 to 15 blankets
- ☐ 10 woolen hats
- ☐ 5 pairs of gloves
- ☐ 5 pairs of mittens
- ☐ 5 scarves

- ☐ 5 winter jackets or coats

To cool your body in the heat
- ☐ 5 squirt bottles
- ☐ 5 cooling towels

PERSONAL HYGIENE
- ☐ 5 toothbrushes (plus extras for guests)
- ☐ 2 (6-ounce [170-g]) tubes of toothpaste
- ☐ 2 containers of dental floss
- ☐ 2 (8-ounce [237-ml]) bottles of shampoo
- ☐ 4 boxes of wet wipes (100 per container)
- ☐ 10 (8-ounce [237-ml]) bottles of hand sanitizer
- ☐ 2 bars of soap
- ☐ 3 (8-ounce [237-ml]) tubes or bottles of hand moisturizer
- ☐ 3 (8-ounce [237-ml]) bottles of body lotion
- ☐ Feminine products if needed
- ☐ 24 cloth diapers if there's a baby in the household

PAPER DISHES
- ☐ 150 of each: paper plates, bowls, and cups
- ☐ 150 of each: plastic forks, knives, and spoons
- ☐ 150 paper napkins
- ☐ 16 rolls of paper towels

CLEANING SUPPLIES
- ☐ 4 boxes of wet wipes (100 count)
- ☐ 1 gallon (3.8 L) of unscented bleach

MISCELLANEOUS
- ☐ 1 multipurpose knife, such as Swiss Army or Leatherman
- ☐ 2 boxes 300-count wooden matches
- ☐ 2 rolls of duct tape (9 mm–2 inches [5 cm] by 60 yards [55 M])

ACKNOWLEDGMENTS

A huge and heartfelt thank you to my husband, Mark, and to my daughters, Alli, Stacie, Heidi, and Camille, my sons-in-law, and my 17 grandchildren. Your love and support mean so much to me, and I am so grateful for your patience with the long hours I spent in front of my computer writing this book. I love you more than words can express.

To my sister, Carol, you've been my cheerleader from the day I started teaching classes, through my ongoing work with my blog *Food Storage Moms*, and now this book. Thank you for always being there for me.

I could not have written this book without Claire Kowalchik and her expert guidance, wisdom, research, and editing. She was patient beyond words and is gifted in so many ways.

Finally, I want to give a big shout-out to my publisher, Will Kiester, and editor, Sarah Monroe, at Page Street Publishing for asking me to write this book and guiding me through the process. Thank you for this awesome opportunity.

ABOUT THE AUTHOR

Linda Loosli is the author of the popular blog *Food Storage Moms* (foodstoragemoms.com). She's been making bread, storing food, and preparing for the unexpected for almost 50 years and has taught classes on these topics for decades. Her blog caught the attention of editors at *The New York Times* who interviewed her after Hurricane Sandy hit the east coast.

With her years of experience and vast expertise, Linda is often asked to speak at events and has consulted with state government agencies as well as private corporations about their emergency-preparedness plans. In addition, several companies that specialize in food storage and emergency supplies—including Goal Zero, The Excalibur Dehydrator Co., Earth Easy, North Bay Trading, Sun Oven, Kelley Kettle, Big Berkey, FoodSaver, Honeyville Grain, and Cox's Honey—regularly reach out to Linda to test new products and demonstrate them to her audience.

Linda lives in southern Utah with her husband, Mark, and is the mother to four daughters and three sons-in-law and grandmother to 17 children.

INDEX